61

MOTIVATIONAL STORIES

FOR EVERY COACH
OF EVERY SPORT

CRAIG FAULKNER,

JOE KOMAROSKI,

AND

RAYMOND SINIBALDI

FOREWORD BY "SKIP" BERTMAN

the Peppertree Press
Sarasota, Florida

Graphic design by Rebecca Barbier.

For information regarding permission,
call 941-922-2662 or contact us at our website:
www.peppertreepublishing.com or write to:
the Peppertree Press, LLC.
Attention: Publisher
1269 First Street, Suite 7
Sarasota, Florida 34236

ISBN: 978-1-61493-435-6

Library of Congress Number: 2016902877

Printed March 2016

DEDICATIONS

Craig— For Betty Jo, where it all begins and ends, for her
unwavering love and support. And to Clint, Bailey
and Carley, the greatest kids in the world.

Joe— For Sue, Nicole, Allie, Drew & Ty;
thank you for letting me go out and play.

Ray— For Rach, Beth, "Boom", "Mook" and "Jules"
my five bright lights and coaches all.

AUTHORS NOTE

Nearly one third of these stories contain Youtube links which can be used to enhance your use of them. The majority run from three to eight minutes with some being longer. Some come from movie clips and others are live clips. All of them will enhance the stories if you choose to use them. Even if you do not show them to your team; watching them yourself will assist you in the telling.

You will also note the length of the story of *The Miracle on Ice*. As we researched and developed the story, it became imminently clear that there truly is no comparable sports story in the entire history of sports competition. The multiple facets to this story provide any coach of any sport with a plethora of opportunities to motivate players and a team at so many different levels. This coupled with the fact that the true meaning of what took place in Lake Placid in 1980 can best be comprehended by an understanding of the historical context in which this game took place. Mindful of this, we took the effort to put forth that explanation.

Lastly, it is important to note, as you read these stories, that our point of reference is baseball. We coach in a high school baseball program. Therefore, when you read our closing paragraphs in these tales to motivate; you will notice we use baseball references and the nouns gentlemen and men. The discernible reader will understand that any of these stories can be used in any sport and will motivate any athlete, male or female.

ACKNOWLEDGEMENTS

This project has been literally decades in the making. In all actuality, it began when Craig stepped on to the baseball field at LSU and his energy converged with the legendary coach and motivator, "Skip" Bertman. Thus we begin with a thank you to "Skip," the grandfather of this project. The impact of your leadership and mentoring continues on. Thanks to Margeaux Sinibaldi for her outstanding editing work. In the true spirit of a team effort, she made us better.

Craig: First I want to acknowledge where it begins for us all, my Mom and Dad for instilling the values, modeling them, and their lifetime of love and support. Pastor Ziegler, Pastor Tom Hodge, Chris Bando, Brother Jim Bain, Don Gordon, ML Woodruff, and John Zeller for your friendship, mentorship and spiritual influence in my life. Joe Komaroski and Ray Sinibaldi, thank you for your inexhaustible support and energy to keep us reaching for the highest levels. And finally to my coaching staff at Venice High School whose immeasurable loyalty is immeasurably appreciated.

Joe: Thank You Craig Faulkner, for letting a guy with no talent play on your team! Thank You Remo Sinibaldi, for without your determined efforts this work never takes flight! Finally, Thank You God, for you continually blessing me beyond my abilities! GtH!

Ray: In the writing of this book the echoes of my yesterdays visited me and I once again was reminded of the great fortune bestowed upon me when Mary Kelly and Remo Sinibaldi brought me into the world. Dad, your words resonate more poignant and clear with the passage of time. To "Pistol" Pete Hunton, my first coach, you are always with me. To my big brother Willie, the grinder who never gives in and Paul, my "Two Stop" buddy and a brother in every sense of the word- his insight and perspective has, more than once, rescued me from the abyss. Joe K and Craig, thanks for showing me my best is yet to come. To the girls of Plant who took me in and give me hope, and to Jake, Addy, Brady, Reagan and Quinn who make the flowers in my heart bloom. And to Lynda…Just because.

Remo Sinibaldi, the elder and wiser, used to say that we come into the world naked and alone and we go out naked and alone; yet in between are relationships, and in those relationships is the measure of the essence of who we are. Craig, Joe and Ray took decidedly different paths that brought them to the baseball fields of Venice High School and the confluence of their energies has worked to bring out the best from each other. It is all about relationships. We are grateful for ours!

FOREWORD

Remember the popular 1970s game show, "Let's Make a Deal?" Monte Hall, the game show host, would show the contestant three doors and they would make a choice to win what's behind door number one, door number two or door number three. In a hypothetical "Let's Make a Deal" to be played by coaches, let's say we know in advance what is behind the three doors. Door number one is "losing most of the games you coach;" obviously no coach wants what's behind that door. Door number two says, the coach will win a large amount of the games they coach. It appears to be a no-brainer with no need to even bother with door number three. But actually what's behind door number three is the best choice for all coaches and it does not matter what sport they coach. Behind door number three it says that the coach and the athletes will try as hard as they can to win each game. That the coach will use the sport to teach life lessons. That the coach will work hard each day to make each athlete a better person both on and off the playing field. It means that putting on a uniform carries with it a history and a commitment. That a player will honor the sports past and the spirit of everyone who has come before them. And perhaps most importantly each coach and player will become an important part of the community in which they play.

It is first important to realize that Craig Faulkner, the baseball coach at Venice High School, chose door number three and for all for the right reasons. First, he knows baseball! After graduating from Venice High School he came to LSU where he played for me for four years. In those four years he was a key component to two trips to Omaha and leading a program to new heights. He then played eight years of minor league baseball before coaching for the Baltimore Orioles AA club in Bowie, Md. Second, he forsook a professional coaching career to return to his home town where he was needed to help his wife with their firstborn baby, Clint, a special needs child born with Down Syndrome. He and his lovely wife Betty Jo, have two other children, Bailey and Carley. He chose door number three because he is a great husband and father as well as an excellent coach.

Coaching is a tough job. You really can't copy a successful coach and there is no secret chemistry that works for all coaches; no one size fits all blueprint for success. The coach is out in the open, easily judged by many who are not qualified to judge. For the coach, there is no place to hide. Coach Craig Faulkner and his staff, (most who have been with him for all 17 years) is one coach who just has "it". A blend of knowledge, temperament, patience and much more.

In those seventeen years as the head coach at Venice High School his teams have won ten District Championships, seven Regional Championships and Four State Championships. Many of his players have gone on to play college baseball and even professional baseball but ALL of his players went on to be better fathers and husbands, great community members and of course the players feel ownership in the program which they helped Coach build. They have labored to create one of the great high school facilities in the country.

An essential component of a coach's success is the ability to motivate. Craig's book of motivational stories, for all occasions, is a wonderful tool for coaches of any sport and also for any manager or leader who wants to motivate their players.

Let me set the stage. After both teams take infield and the field is being readied for the game which is 10 or 15 minutes away; Craig takes his team to the outfield where the players encircle him and he awaits eye contact from everyone. This is a great moment of readiness to learn, the players are intense, yet they have a few minutes to relax.

Coach begins his story. Never the same one used twice in one year. For example, if the focus is on breaking any mental barrier, (breaking a bad streak, or continuing a winning streak) he will tell his team about Roger Bannister breaking the barrier of the four minute mile. If he wants a quick pregame story before a big game he can go to "Be a Jewel, Thrive on the Heat and Pressure of Competition". There are many pregame stories used to keep your team focused in the moment, winning the small battles; one pitch at a time, one play at a time, one point at a time.

Craig uses the stories pregame and during the week. He researches to get his dates and facts right and he is ready to deliver the life lesson in each particular required instance. His preparation allows him to deliver his message with conviction! If the team is not bringing all they should to practice he will explain the need to stay sharp with the "Slicing Tomatoes" story. If players need to make an adjustment he may tell them about Steve Carlton or Sandy Koufax. A story needed about defending home turf will call for the "Our Chips" story or perhaps the tale of "Lions and Tigers and Bears." A big game story may call for "Ali's Rope a Dope" or "Eating an Elephant" and a simple story of believing in yourself will have him telling his players the story of Doug Flutie or Jim Abbott. The stories of Dan Marino or Ken Brett will help the team embrace those great moments of post season play.

Short stories work! Many of my players remember a story I told at LSU before a game or during practice! Whether it's business or baseball or any sport; the stories are wonderful at team building, point making, breaking tension, building confidence, moving towards excellence and of course, motivation.

They are all here for the coach, the board room, the pulpit or the classroom, Craig's laid the groundwork for you to build on!

Craig has gained respect with a very simple method, personal example. He's worked harder, been more dedicated, concerned, loyal, meticulous and enthusiastic than most of the other people I have watched work at their baseball jobs.

In the end Craig Faulkner is simply a winner in every way. When he played he was the player I wanted up in the ninth inning of a close game. He's the guy a basketball coach would want to take the last shot of the game.

The truth is, as a player, Craig Faulkner always came through, as a coach, he always comes through and it's no surprise in this, his first book, he's come through again!

Skip Bertman

CONTENTS

CHAPTER TWO
THE MIND OF THE COMPETITOR   68

CHAPTER THREE
ADVERSITY—IT HITS ALL PLAYERS AND ALL TEAMS   89

INTRODUCTION

If Craig Faulkner is the father of this project then there can be no doubt that the legendary Skip Bertman is indeed the grandfather. The paths of these two great baseball minds crossed in 1984 when Faulkner walked in to Alex Box Stadium at Louisiana State University.

A 1983 graduate of Venice (FL) High School, Faulkner was a three-letter athlete having played basketball, football and baseball. However, it was baseball that was his calling and the 6'5" 215 lb. catcher wanted to become a Tiger.

Bertman, who played at the University of Miami, came to Baton Rouge after serving as an assistant on the staff of his alma mater. The confluence of these two energies began a transformation of the baseball culture at LSU, which today is among the most powerfully successful college baseball programs in the country.

Baseball began on the campus of LSU in 1893 and in their first 30 years of existence, 15 coaches were at the helm until Harry Rabenhorst took over in 1927. Rabenhorst piloted the Tigers until 1956 except for three years where he served his country in WWII. During his tenure came the construction of the LSU Varsity Field, two SEC Titles, and two SEC Coach of the Year honors. In 1943 the field was officially dedicated Alex Box Stadium in honor of the LSU alumnus who was killed in action in North Africa in 1942.

Four different men led the Tigers during the next 28 years, bringing but two more conference championships. And then Bertman arrived and so did a kid named Faulkner.

J. Stanley "Skip" Bertman was a three time Florida High School Coach of the Year and a National Champion as an assistant under Ron Fraser at Miami before taking the head coaching job at LSU. He would hold the position for 18 seasons compiling a record of 870-330-3. The Tigers qualified for the NCAA post season tournament in 16 of those 18 seasons winning seven SEC titles and appearing in the College World Series 11 times. In those 11 appearances they emerged five times as the National Champions. In 2008 a new stadium was built on the campus of LSU. It is located on Skip Bertman Drive and it bears the name Alex Box Stadium/Skip Bertman Field.

Craig Faulkner was a force for positive change of the LSU culture. A member of Bertman's first team he played on the 1986 SEC Champions and also on LSU's first College World Series team. A natural leader Faulkner was both the captain and MVP of the Tiger's 1987 squad.

He played eight years in the organizations of the Baltimore Orioles, Milwaukee Brewers and the St. Louis Cardinals and in 1997, he found himself back at Venice High School where he was an assistant coach for two seasons before taking the top spot in 1999.

Using Bertman's model at LSU, Faulkner established a motto of "Excellence On and Off the Field" and it has been the stamp upon Venice High School Baseball for nearly two decades. In 2016 he will enter his 18th year as head coach and on the field his team has compiled a record of 352-156, with 10 district championships, seven regional championships and four state championships. He is a four-time Florida Coach of the Year (twice in 7A and once each in 6A and 5A) and he was named Florida Dairy Farmers High School Baseball Coach of the Year; a statewide honor, in 2015. Three times the Florida Athletic Coaches Association has named him head coach of the state of Florida's prep all-star team.

Off the field his teams have, in nearly two decades of giving back, compiled approximately 25,000 hours of service to the community of Venice, Florida. It is a wide range of community endeavors the young men of the baseball team reach and they include but are not limited to; reading mentors for elementary students, visiting the elderly in local nursing homes, Habitat for Humanity, Little League Baseball Challenger Program and an annual night each season in which the players participate in honoring America's veterans. And three of his teams have won the Florida State Championship for team GPA.

In 2011, he joined with childhood friend, Venice High teammate and LSU teammate Mark Guthrie to form the Florida Burn; a travel ball program that quickly rose to become one of the most elite travel ball teams in the country. Guthrie's 15 years in the major leagues combined with Faulkner's playing and coaching prowess rocketed the Burn to their elite status. The program has assisted hundreds of Florida high school student athletes achieve their dreams of taking their game to the next level. And along the way they learn the game of baseball, in the words of a wide range of college coaches, "the right way."

Skip Berman was such a force and source of inspiration in Craig Faulkner's life, and his motivational stories were so powerful that Faulkner has used many of them, built upon others, and for three decades, chronicled, compiled and written scores more. Alumni have returned to Faulkner with their own tales of how some of these stories have been remembered and used to motivate them far beyond the baseball field.

Finally, he has collaborated with Venice High staff members Joe Komaroski and Ray Sinibaldi to put those stories to pen. Over 60 of them are contained herein and each story is begun with a short explanation as to how they can be applied. Of course you will add to them, modify, structure, and apply them to the individual needs and challenges your individual players and team face throughout the season. They encompass virtually all of the challenges a coach will encounter in their efforts to get the best from their players and bring them together as a team.

A THEME FOR ALL SEASONS
SETTING THE TONE
FOR THE YEAR

The challenge of every coach is to motivate their players on a day to day, game to game, week to week basis. All coaches are aware of the variables which can affect any team; some foreseeable, many not. Each team, each season will develop a life of its own and it is the job of the coaching staff to respond to all the events which will effect that team. This tome is replete with stories involving the plethora of challenges which can and will unfold.

Many of these challenges can be anticipated and addressed before the season even begins. This chapter outlines some seasonal themes that have been very effective in first setting a tone for the season, guiding a team to finding its identity, and implementing both short and long term goals for the season.

There are occasions when a motivating story at some point in time during the season grows and becomes a rallying cry and focal point for the team; thus turning into a theme which the team itself adopts on their own. They have been included in this chapter as well.

CHAPTER ONE

THE TEAM:
BUILDING, BONDING, DEFINING

1. TRUST

CHARLES BLONDIN AND HARRY COLCORD

This story can either be a practice story early in the season to build trust or during the season when you sense that trust may be eroding. It can also be used in a pregame situation as well.

He was born Jean-Francois Gravelet in Pas-De-Calais, France in 1824 and was an accomplished acrobat by the age of five. He was nicknamed "Blondin" because of his fair hair and by five he was also known as the "Little Wonder." When he arrived in the United States in 1855. he was known as Charles Blondin.

In the summer of 1859, Blondin became the first man to walk across Niagara Falls on a tightrope. Using the local Niagara Falls Gazette to promote his intent, other newspapers began to pick up the story and soon Blondin's escapades became a national phenomenon as people, across the land, began following the exploits of "The Great Blondin." *The New York Times* stated he ought to be arrested, but Blondin was undaunted. He knew his capabilities, he trusted his instincts and he trusted his ability. People began to flock to the falls as railroad companies ran specials to Niagara Falls. Throughout the summer he made the 1100 foot journey, on the three-inch cable, 160 feet over the raging falls in a myriad of different ways: he traversed it blindfolded, pushed a wheelbarrow, he stopped and cooked an omelet, he crossed it on stilts, he rode a bike, and once crossed with his hands and legs bound in chains. Another time he dressed in a gorilla costume for the 10 to 15 minute stroll over the mist of the great Niagara. He never once doubted his ability to make the trip safely for his trust in himself was unshakable!

However nobody could anticipate what was about to take place one late afternoon on August 19, 1859. A huge crowd of over 25,000 had gathered to watch the "Great Blondin" and they were abuzz with anticipation. It was 5:15 PM and bands played on both sides of the river as Blondin began his walk. Halfway through he paused, lay down and rested for five minutes or so before he rose to his feet and finished the task. The crowd cheered wildly as the bands kept playing. Responding to his enthusiastic reception, Blondin employed the crowd, "Do you believe I could do this with a man on my back?" "Yes", the crowd responded. "Do you believe?" he implored again and the crowd shouted back, "Yes we believe!" "Who of you will volunteer?" he shouted and a hush fell over the crowd. "Well" he exhorted the crowd and all that could be heard was the water from the Niagara River crashing down 160 feet to the rocks below.

Suddenly a man began to move through the crowd, and as he made his way into the open, all eyes were upon him. "Me, I Believe and I will do it." A great roar went up from the gathering as Harry Colcord moved toward the top of the falls and his destiny. Carrying Harry piggyback style, Blondin made his way safely across the tightrope to the delirious cheering of the 25,000 strong gathered below.

Harry Colcord was Charles Blondin's manager. They had worked together for years and in fact, they had practiced tightrope walking with Harry on Charles' back. Harry knew every nuance of his friend and trusted him impeccably. He had no hesitations about placing his life in the hands, or on the back of Charles Blondin. And Charles trusted that Harry would not panic, would not falter, and would not waver! This duo put their lives into the hands of each other. No trust is more complete!

Many of us have been here two, three or four years. We have learned to trust one another and play as a team. We have learned to trust the coaches and to trust the system. We have learned to believe in one another. We have worked hard to learn to trust ourselves and to place that trust in the hands of your teammates.

Tonight trust your skills and the skills of your teammates! Trust that if you boot the ball your pitcher will pick you up. Trust that if you give up a couple of runs, your teammates will score and get you back in it! Play hard, play intelligently and play together!

https://www.youtube.com/watch?v=6wATDb8KJWQ

2. PROTECT YOUR TURF
—HOME GAME

LIONS AND TIGERS AND BEARS, OH MY!

A pregame story when a formidable opponent is visiting your home.

Lions, Tigers, Bears and Wolves have ruled the wilderness since its creation! Man has feared these predators since man became a part of that wilderness. Lions, Tigers, Wolves and Bears are the stuff of which nightmares are made. Despite technology and weaponry nothing will strike more fear in the human heart. They work alone or in packs with no limits to their time spent hunting when they are hungry. They possess the teeth, strength, agility and tenacity to hunt down the most cunning prey and claim them with one bite to the jugular or a single swipe of a massive claw.

These beastly predators have been researched for decades both in the wild and in captivity; unveiling a remarkable fact- Lions, tigers, bears and wolves not only hunt and not only kill for food, they destroy their enemies for two reasons; Hunger and Territory!

It is easy to understand that all species must eat to sustain life. But, what is shocking is that these animals' number one motivation to savagely attack and kill is their overwhelming desire to PROTECT THEIR TERRITORY! No man is safe when they have stumbled upon the turf of these dangerous beasts of prey; regardless of time of day or night, regardless of weather, these beast will fight to the death to defend their turf.

"Tonight we may be content and void of any real hunger, but someone has stumbled onto our turf. We must be tenacious, unyielding and angry in our defense of our environment. We must be prepared, we must lurk and we must devour this enemy who has dared to tread upon our turf.

We are not hungry and we take no pleasure in fighting but, we will defend our field like we are a pack of wild beasts. We will be unmatched in our passion to defend.

No man is safe in our jungle tonight!"

3. BENT NICKEL

WEEDING OUT THE MALCONTENT

This is a team building exercise and is best used in a classroom setting with the "visual aids".

This is a hands on team building exercise. Take 20 nickels and bend two or three of them with a vice. Give each player a nickel and have them stack them asking the players which is the most important. Begin stacking the nickels, beginning with all the flat ones. As you are stacking them, explain that each team has a belief system in place and that the key to implementing that belief system is trust. "We must trust in the system and in each other."

Take down the stack and begin anew. Only this time introduce the bent nickels and when you place it in the stack focus on the bent nickel. Ask the question, "Can a bent out of shape person who has lost his belief in the system and in his teammates carry anyone else?" After a few flat nickels, add a bent one and say, maybe a couple and add the bent ones toward the bottom of the pile saying, "Eventually, it will all break down." Stack the nickels until they tumble.

As the stack gets higher and near the top, explain that if a player's belief in the system is absent, or broken, that player can only be carried BY THE TEAM! Place the bent nickels at the top to illustrate the point.

Gentlemen, it only takes one or two players who lose their faith in the system, their trust in their teammates or to get lost in their own selfish pursuits and the team can falter.

An individual can never stack their nickels fast enough, or work hard enough or sincere enough to make up for a bent nickel belief. It must be 100% commitment to and belief in the system. It makes no difference if the player is a starter, manager, or a role player we will never stack fast enough to overcome bent players.

Your belief system shapes your life, it is who and what we are, or what we will become. It is a collective responsibility of every teammate, every coach to seek out and spend time with the bent player.

Men, baseball is the greatest of games and one reason is because there is always several options at a coach's disposal; from the selection of players in the lineup to the many situations which arise during a game. These decisions are always open to second guessing and review. Do not let these decisions cause a bend in your nickel. Keep it flat, stay the course, believe in our objective, trust our system. The team needs you, all of you and do not lose sight of the fact that you are a part of something that is bigger than you, bigger than any one individual on this team. Stay in the moment and step by step we will achieve our goal.

4. ULTIMATE TEAM PLAYER

DREW BLEDSOE / TOM BRADY

This is an outstanding story of self-sacrifice and putting the team ahead of individual pursuits. A practice story for sure!

Drew Bledsoe was first overall pick of the New England Patriots in the 1993 draft. In his ninth season with New England he had quite an impressive resume. He was the youngest quarterback in NFL history to make the Pro Bowl (a three time electee) and to surpass 10,000 yards in passing. In 1994 he led the league in passing yards and became the second NFL quarterback to complete 400 passes in a season. He had seven consecutive seasons with 3000 plus yards passing and he held the Patriot record of 179 consecutive passes without an interception. Four times in his first six seasons he led New England to the playoffs including a Super Bowl appearance in 1996. And in March of 2001 he had signed a contract for 102 million dollars, surpassing Brett Favre as the highest paid player in the NFL.

Tom Brady was a sixth round New England draft pick out of Michigan in the 2000 draft. The overall 199th player chosen.

It was game two of the 2001 season and the New York Jets were in Foxboro battling the Patriots and New England was 0-1. Bledsoe was injured running around right end when he was blasted out of bounds by Jets linebacker Mo Lewis. Many on the New England sidelines called it the loudest hit they've ever heard.

Tom Brady took the field with exactly THREE plays of experience! Brady ran 11 plays, completing five of ten passes for 46 yards and running once for a nine yard gain. However, the game ended on the Jets 29 and the Patriots were on the short end of a 10-3 score.

Bledsoe, meanwhile was in an ambulance with a sheered blood vessel in his chest, his lung filling with blood causing it to collapse. His brother was at his side as the star quarterback was drifting in and out of consciousness. His life was now in danger. Mass General doctor David Berger said he had "never seen an injury like this in a professional athlete."

It was the 15th game of the season and Drew Bledsoe was medically cleared to play. Eschewing the old adage that a player never loses his starting spot due to injury, Patriots head coach Bill Belichick stuck with Brady at quarterback.

Much of what followed is well known. The "Tuck Rule" game against Oakland and the Super Bowl win, the first for Tom Brady and the New England Patriots. What is not as well-known is the controversy created in the AFC Championship game.

It was played at Heinz Field in Pittsburg and the Steelers were 10 point favorites. With 1:59 left in the first half and New England ahead 7-3 Tom Brady rolled his ankle and had to leave the game; enter Drew Bledsoe. In four plays, Bledsoe had the Patriots in the end zone finishing the drive with an 11 yard touchdown pass and with Drew Bledsoe at the helm throughout the second half, the Patriots prevailed 24-17 and were bound for the Super Bowl.

With only one week until the Super Bowl, the media wondered; "Would Bledsoe or Brady start the Super Bowl?" It was late Wednesday when Coach Bill Belichick announced that Brady was healthy and would start the Super Bowl.

So Drew Bledsoe, the best quarterback in the history of the New England franchise and the highest paid player in the NFL; participated from the sidelines as Tom Brady led the Patriots to their first Super Bowl victory, earning game MVP honors along the way!

Through what was the most difficult season in Drew Bledsoe's exceptional career, a season which saw him go from Pro Bowl superstar to backup, he never lost sight of the team's ultimate objective…TO WIN!!!

He could have groused about why he should have been the starter and there were many who would have agreed with him. He could have chosen the selfish road, made it all about how unfair it was to him and become a negative force and distraction.

He didn't. Instead he became a mentor to the young quarterback doing everything he could to make Tom Brady the best he could be. And when all was said and done this is what he had to say, "As hard as it was to stand there and watch somebody else on the field, it was very gratifying to see one of the truly good guys be rewarded for all of the hard work and dedication that he showed."

Drew Bledsoe...The Ultimate Teammate!!!!

Every player who competes faces this possibility. Every player must examine their motives and ask themselves, "What are you doing each day to make yourself better? What are you doing each day to make your team better? Do you have to be the reason we win a championship or is winning the championship enough?"

It is you who decides how to handle it, what energy to give it and how to help the team. Brady gave a tremendous amount of credit to Drew Bledsoe for his success then and throughout his entire career.

When you are faced with this choose Drew Bledsoe's way... The team needs that from you!

5. DOG SOLDIERS

WHO WILL STAKE HIS CLAIM

This is a story of looking after and standing by each other. It is about picking each other up and coming together for the tough battle that awaits; a pregame story.

There is no experience that will bind people together like the experience of combat. To place your life in someone else's hands and have them place their life in yours is as deep an emotional and spiritual occurrence that a human can encounter in their lifetime.

History is replete with stories of men in combat who have endured unfathomable difficulties to fight and protect their brothers in arms. None braver, more courageous, or tenacious than the Cheyenne "Dog Soldier."

It was the Cheyenne who defeated Custer under Crazy Horse at Little Big Horn; fighting with a ferocity which decimated Custer's 7th US Calvary. They were as well respected a warrior that has ever fought. They were devoted to the protection of their fellow warriors with a custom which is unmatched in the annals of combat.

Each soldier carried a "dog rope" and attached to each rope was a spear. The spear was driven into the battleground, literally staking the Dog Soldier to the ground as a mark of their resolve in combat; a working symbol of their devotion to their brothers in battle. They would not leave the battle field until every brother warrior was safe. He would not relent nor retreat.

Often the shear sight of the warrior driving his stake or clanking sound of the driven stake would instill fear in the hearts of opponents.

We face a tough battle tonight men, it is a noble, hard fighting opponent we face. Who of you is going to be our Dog Soldier? Who among you will drive their stake first? Who among you is going to be the one to stake his claim to this battle ground and not waver, fight to the end and never retreat?

For one or more of you, tonight is your time!

6. FINISH THE JOB

THERE IS STILL WORK TO DO

This is a story for a situation where you have had a big win but there is still a way to go before your objective of a district title or league championship is realized.

It was May 8, 1945 when WW II in Europe finally came to an end. Eight days earlier Adolf Hitler committed suicide in his Berlin bunker and thus the burden of surrender fell to German President Karl Donitz. Donitz signed two surrender documents, one in France on May 7th and the following day in Berlin. Needless to say, there was unbounded joy and celebration throughout Europe which had been at war for the better part of a decade.

There were 3,000,000 American soldiers serving in Europe, at the time. However, for 1,000,000 of them the war was not over. The celebration was short lived and they had to refocus their efforts to fight!

With fierce fighting still raging in the Pacific, these 1,000,000 men were placed on transport ships and sent to the Pacific to prepare for the final invasion of Japan. Many of these men had fought in North Africa, Italy, France, Belgium and Germany.

We have battled all season, and our hard work and focus has brought us to this point! We have achieved a lot and we have successes in which we are proud. We cannot afford to let down, our celebration is over and we must refocus! For if we do not reach our goal and accomplish our objective, we will diminish what we have already achieved. Stay the course men! Maintain the focus, for despite our success the job is not finished. Tonight we face an opponent who wants to derail our season. Tonight men we become like those brave men of 70 years ago, war weary, tired and ready to do whatever is necessary to finish the job!

Let's go take it!!!!

7. HARNESS THE HORSES

WORKING TOGETHER

This is a practice story for early in the season as it illustrates the point that the goal and desire of each "horse" needs to be to pull in the same direction with the team's success the priority. It's about the whole being greater than the sum of the individual parts.

Back in the days of Christ, the chariot races were the most popular form of entertainment. People would flock to the coliseums to watch and to bet on the teams. The teams were comprised of four horses pulling the chariot driven by a single man. Legend has it that one of the most successful teams was owned by an Arab Sheik. Four brilliant white Arabian stallions driven by a Jewish Prince named Judah.

The original team of horses were named Mera, Altair, Aldebaran and Rigel. The fastest and strongest of the four was Mera. However Mera could not conform to the other three and invariably would pull them off course, fight them on the turns and thus the team could not succeed. The decision was made to replace Mera with another horse, Antares. Although Antares was not as strong nor as fast as Mera, the team began to win! Antares appeared to have an innate understanding of working as a unit and in fact with her, the team was faster, stronger and more disciplined. After Antares joined the team, they never lost another race. For seven years until Judah stopped racing they were UNDEFEATED!

When horses are being chosen for a team, it is not always the size, the strength or the speed. We are looking for the horses that work together for the good of the team. When a team of horses are pulling in the same direction it is nice to watch, it can look almost poetic. They make it seem effortless as they get the most from each individually and pull the most and best from each other. Again, it does not have to be the biggest, the fastest or the strongest, it has to be the horses that are willing to have the mentality to conform to the unit, to believe in the objective, to give their individual best, pull the same direction as the others and make them better.

What would it look like if one of the horses pulled in a different direction? Chaos would ensue and it would become extremely difficult to run the race. How can a horse work in the wrong direction, against the team? Late to weight training, disrespectful of coaches, poor off field behavior, players who put themselves above the team. How does the trainer get the horse to pull in the right direction? With discipline, training and preparedness he works to unify the horse's efforts. But above all it is the horse that must buy in, trust the trainer and the horses that he runs with.

Men we need to harness our efforts. We want all horses pulling in the same direction for we know that it is essential to our success. However we also know that there are some horses that refuse to become part of the team effort and it is at that point that we will have to make the decision to remove him, even if he is the most powerful of horses.

https://www.youtube.com/watch?v=frE9rXnaHpE

ꟻ

8. HONKERS AND WINDBREAKERS

EVERYONE TAKES A TURN AT LEADERSHIP

This is a story of team unity, picking each other up and individuals stepping up to leadership roles. A nice pregame story to use imploring players to pick each other up and can also be used in practice as well.

We all have seen geese flying across the sky in their strictly patterned "V" formation. How often have we paused and simply asked "why do they do that?" and more importantly, "How do they know to do it?" Scientist have explained the purpose and value of such a plan as the "V" formation.

The purpose of the formation is to form a wall to block the wind and lessen the group's overall effort to fly through the air. The lead goose faces the wind head on, diminishing its power and swirl making it easier for the remaining geese in formation. Birds, who fly behind the leader, fight lesser tide of air enabling them to last longer and fly further.

Flying against the wind saps the energy of the leader and he is thus incapable of leading for the entire journey. A flock, needing to travel fast to survive, will easily wear out one front-flyer after another. However the mass of birds recognize the value of the windbreakers and use a method to rally the head goose to stay in the line longer – they honk.

Honking is not done to catch the attention of humans, but is intended to express appreciation and encouragement to the one goose that is facing the wind on behalf of the others. The louder they honk, the longer the leader will be inspired to keep fighting through the wind.

When the first leader finally wears out and drops back to assume a different role, he will honk to help new leaders who move out front.

Throughout any given season, any given game each of you will have an opportunity to be a windbreaker and a honker. Like the flock of geese we are a unit! Each playing a role and supporting each other in that role. Together, honkers and wind breakers bring the flock home!

Remember, even though geese fly in formation, each is responsible for their own landing. Until then, everyone counts on everyone else. Each has a role.

Tonight, play "your role" and encourage others when you should. When you are out front know that the rest of the team is pulling for you. If you are in the background pull for the guys out front. Let's win as a team!

9. PLAY FOR SOMEONE ELSE

LOU LITTLE / LUIGI PICCOLO

This is a story that can be used either in practice or in a pregame situation. It is a call to get the best from your players and to do it in an unselfish manner; do it for someone else.

Luigi Piccolo was an All-American football player at Pennsylvania College in 1916. After fighting in WWI he became a legendary coach first at the prestigious colleges of Georgetown (1924-1929) and Columbia University (1930-1956). He was elected to the College Football Hall of Fame in 1960. The son of Italian immigrants, Luigi did what many immigrants did at that time; he anglicized his name and became known as Lou Little.

In his 20 plus years as a coach, he often told the story of his all-time favorite player, a young man named John. John did not possess a lot of physical athletic talent, was not all that fast or quick. However, John worked as hard as any player he'd ever coached, and was perhaps the greatest team player he ever saw. He never played all that much but Coach Little would work him into a game whenever he could. John would often go weeks without seeing the field and he once went an entire season without playing a down.

John's father came to every single game, even though John rarely played. Coach would see John walking on campus arm in arm with his father. Obviously, they were very close. He would see them in the cafeteria and praying together in the Chapel. Late in the season during John's senior season, Little received a call that John's father had passed away. John's mom asked Coach Little to tell John the news. "He thinks the world of you Coach", she said "I would appreciate it coming from you." The toughest day in this coach's life was when he found John and summoned him to his office to break the bad news. John took the news as well as to be expected and Coach helped make the arrangements to get him home. "Take all the time you need John," Coach told him and he expected he may not see him again. At least until the season ended.

A week later, Coach Little saw John walking alone on campus. Coach approached him and asked how he was getting along. John said that he and his family were doing okay. Coach Little said; "If there was anything I can do for you, please let me know." "Coach," John said through a cracking voice, "I would like to start this Saturday in the homecoming game against Georgetown." Coach looked at John, "I'll tell you what John, when we take the field you will be out there on the first set of downs, that's all I can promise you." "That's fine," said John and he thanked him and they parted.

The game began with John at linebacker. (In those days, most guys played both ways.) On the first play, John broke through the offensive line and tackled the ball carrier for a loss. Coach Little smiled. He made tackles on the next two plays so Coach let him remain in the game on the offensive side of the ball. Sure enough, he opened two holes there as well. This went on the entire day, he ran up and down the field and played like and All-American. Columbia won, John was given the game ball and named the game MVP. Later in the locker room celebration, Coach Little noticed John, alone, head bowed and visibly crying. Coach sat next to him and put his arm around him. John gathered himself and Coach said, "John that was the most remarkable athletic endeavor I have ever witnessed. You were spectacular out there, where did that come from?" "Coach", John replied, "today was the first game my father ever saw me play." Coach Little was puzzled. 'John, I know you never got in all that much, but your dad was at every game, he saw you out there." "Coach, my dad was blind. Today I knew he would be able to see me play. Today I played this game for him." John looked at Coach Little with tears in his eyes, "Thanks Coach, thanks for the chance". "No son," replied Coach Little, "thank you."

Gentlemen, someone sitting in those stands tonight will be watching you play for the first time. Take John's lead and tonight play like an All American. Play this game for someone else; for someone in your family, someone who loves you and supports you each day like John's father did for him.

10. SLICING TOMATOES

DON'T GO THROUGH THE MOTIONS IN PRACTICE
STAY SHARP

This is a practice story to use when the team is not bringing all they should to practice. It may be after a couple of wins against weaker teams and you sense the team losing some of its intensity, growing a bit complacent. We used this one time when our team had started the season 8-0. Following a couple of "lackluster" wins we saw a slip in intensity. The team rebounded winning another eight straight before falling to the number one team in the state.

Men, have you ever cut through a tomato with a sharp knife? If you have, you know it's easy, if you haven't trust us, it's very easy. In fact, you will be able to cut through tomato after tomato and the funny thing is, you will not even notice that the knife is growing dull. That won't happen until you attempt to cut a nice piece of juicy steak!

The last few teams we've played have really been tomatoes. We've been able to cut through them even as our knives have become a bit dull. There are a couple of juicy steaks looming in our not too distant future and if we use this dull knife we've been carrying around our last few practices, we will have a very difficult time getting through those sirloins.

It is imperative that we take the time to sharpen our knife after every tomato we slice. When we keep a high focus, give our best effort and approach practice with the proper level of intensity, we are sharpening our knives.

Let's sharpen our knives today at practice. Let's get them so sharp that we slice those steaks coming up with the same smoothness that we sliced those tomatoes!

11. ASK NOT

WHAT CAN I DO FOR THIS TEAM?

This is a preseason story as you set the tone for unselfish play. It highlights a mindset of team first and helps illustrate the importance of channeling energy to making the team better; not individual pursuits. A team theme can be referenced throughout the season and built upon throughout the year.

It was January 20, 1961 and it was a clear, cold day in Washington DC with about a foot of new snow on the ground as the crowds gathered around the steps of the US Capitol building. Shortly after noontime, 43 year old John F. Kennedy took the oath of office as the 35th President of the United States.

In his inaugural address he outlined what would later be dubbed his "New Frontier". It was a perilous time for the United States. The Cold War was simmering, the Russians had surpassed the US in rocket technology that many thought shifted the balance of power in the Soviets favor. He summed up the perilous times early in his speech. "The world is very different now. For man holds in his mortal hands the power to abolish all forms of human poverty and all forms of human life. And yet the same revolutionary beliefs for which our forebears fought are still at issue around the globe--the belief that the rights of man come not from the generosity of the state but from the hand of God."

Undaunted, Kennedy outlined the tone of his administration by explaining what he had vowed in his acceptance speech by outlining "not what I intend to offer the American people…..but what I intend to ask of them" that his New Frontier was "not a set of promises…… but it is a set of challenges."

He set the country on a course, challenging Americans. "In your hands, my fellow citizens, more than mine, will rest the final success or failure of our course. Since this country was founded, each generation of Americans has been summoned to give testimony to its national loyalty. The graves of young Americans who answered the call to service surround the globe. Now the trumpet summons us again-not as a call to bear arms, though arms we need--not as a call to battle, though embattled we are--but a call to bear the burden of a long twilight struggle, year in and year out...... Will you join in that historic effort?"

His speech built to a crescendo and it culminated in his expectations for the American people. "In the long history of the world, only a few generations have been granted the role of defending freedom in its hour of maximum danger. I do not shrink from this responsibility--I welcome it. I do not believe that any of us would exchange places with any other people or any other generation. The energy, the faith, the devotion which we bring to this endeavor will light our country and all who serve it--and the glow from that fire can truly light the world.

And so, my fellow Americans: **ask not what your country can do for you--ask what you can do for your country."**

He concluded his speech by urging one and all to," ask of us here the same high standards of strength and sacrifice which we ask of you. With a good conscience our only sure reward, with history the final judge of our deeds, let us go forth to lead the land we love, asking His blessing and His help, but knowing that here on earth God's work must truly be our own."

Gentlemen, this season is going to be a battle. It will be a set of incredible challenges which will push us to the brink. We cannot survive if we are going to allow ourselves to be caught up in our own selfish pursuits. If we have the mind set of what this team can do for me, what you as an individual can take from this team. We are in this together men and you need to ask yourselves, not what this team can do for you but what you can do for this team. Pick up the challenge men, how can you make us better? We approach this game and play like that.....We all win!

https://www.youtube.com/watch?v=mxa4HDgfWFs

12. HOLD THE ROPE

EVERYONE MATTERS

This story can either be used just before the season starts or before a game where it becomes applicable; preferably early in the season. A rope should be used as a visual aid can be effective in the telling of this story and it should be held in front of the group or dangled over a desk.

After presenting the rope you choose a player and ask this question; "If you were dangling off the end of a cliff and holding on to this rope, which player on this team would you choose to have holding the other end?" You add the caveat, "Remember you must choose someone who you know would not ever let you go; no matter how tired he got or how much pain they had to endure."

It is most likely that they will choose the biggest and strongest kid on the team. They will also probably take some time looking about as they decide whom they would choose. It does not really matter who they choose because your response will always be the same. "Men when you do not hesitate in your response to that question and you can simply and unequivocally state;" **It does not matter who holds the rope as long as it is one of my teammates, I don't care who it is, I know none of them will let me fall.**" It is then and only then that we will be where we need to be as a unit, as a team.

This is the kind of trust we must develop among us. It must be unwavering, it must be complete and it requires 100% commitment from each and every one of us. Trust is not something we can buy, it is not something we get from last year's team; rather it's something we earn, earning from each other day in and day out. Players earn it from coaches, coaches earn it from players and players earn it from each other. We will succeed only when each member of the team is trusted.

We earn it, one from each other, by putting the needs of the team ahead of all else. We earn it with an attitude that says simply, what can I do to make **US BETTER?** Gentlemen we are a family and from this day forward we will treat each other as such both on and off the field.

13. WE SHALL NOT BE DERAILED

APOLLO I— REFOCUS AFTER A TOUGH LOSS.

"If we die we want people to accept it. We are in a risky business, and we hope that if anything happens to us, it will not delay the program. The conquest of space is worth the risk of life." —Gus Grissom

This is a story about staying the course and can be used when your team has taken a few lumps and is struggling through some difficulties. It is a story of staying the course and keeping your eye on the objective.

On May 25, 1961, in a speech before the United States Congress, President John F. Kennedy set the United States on a mission. He outlined it with these words, "I believe this nation should commit itself to achieving the goal, before this decade is out, of landing a man on the moon and return him safely to earth." It was 20 days after America's first manned space flight.

NASA's course was now set with a three part program to fulfill this goal. The first part was called Mercury, then Gemini, and finally the moon missions of the Apollo program. President Kennedy would live only long enough to see the Mercury phase come to fruition, the last flight of which took place in May of 1963, six months before his death.

From March of 1965 until November of 1966, 10 Gemini flights were launched with each one building upon the previous one as the United States was literally taking a step by step journey to fulfill President Kennedy's goal. With the Gemini flights successfully completed, the final moon phase awaited, it was time for Apollo.

Apollo I was a scheduled flight of up to two weeks. Their mission was to orbit the earth conducting tests of the command module which would ultimately take Americans to the moon. On January 27, 1967, command pilot Gus Grissom, senior pilot Ed White and pilot Roger Chafee sat in the capsule of the Apollo I spacecraft. During this launch pad test, a voltage spike began a fire in the oxygen-filled capsule. The three astronauts were dead in 15 seconds. Grissom, White and Chafee were the first casualties of the United States Space Program.

NASA was devastated by the loss of the three men and there was some talk of scuttling the idea. However, the decision was made to persevere and efforts were redoubled to fulfill President Kennedy's goal. A completely redesigned command module was put in place and by October of 1968, Apollo VII put the US back in space. Two months later, the crew of Apollo VIII became the first men to orbit the moon and on July 20, 1969 Neil Armstrong took "One small step for man…One giant leap for mankind." Mission accomplished!

The enormity of the loss of these men put a pall over the American space program. It nearly derailed all the efforts and previous successes. It ultimately led to deeper commitment, a new resolve and an unwavering effort to accomplish the objective.

Men we have taken our lumps recently. We have had some hard luck, suffered some tough losses and struggled to find our bearings. But, we cannot relent, we cannot submit, we will not allow ourselves to be swallowed up and scuttle this season. Tonight we rededicate ourselves to our effort and to our objectives. Tonight men, we take step one in turning this around!

https://www.youtube.com/watch?v=b9j2kOcqo78

https://www.youtube.com/watch?v=V0W9bQ2Jg3A

https://www.youtube.com/watch?v=cS8Flvk6dLg

SOURCE:

Gemini : A Personal Account of Man's Venture Into Space (1968) by Virgil I. Grissom

14. PICKING EACH OTHER UP

CURT SCHILLING

This is a story to use when you encounter the player who calls out a teammate for an error or a strikeout or failing to execute at the plate. Or a pitcher who is not making his pitches.

It was the second game of the 2004 World Series. The Red Sox were leading the Cardinals one game to none having won game one 11-9. They were working towards their first World Series win since 1918 and they had just recently vanquished the New York Yankees to win the American League pennant. That was accomplished by becoming the first baseball team in history to be down three games to none in a seven game series and come back to win it. A week earlier Schilling had entered the annals of baseball lore when he limped his way to victory to defeat the Yankees in game six of the ALCS!

With the Red Sox leading 4-1 in the sixth inning, Scott Rolen came to the plate. There were two outs and nobody on when Rolen hit a routine ground ball to third baseman Bill Mueller. It was Mueller's third error of the night! Jim Edmonds followed and reached on an error by the second baseman. This brought the tying run to the plate in the person of Reggie Sanders. Schilling, showed no emotion, he got the ball back and went back to work. He got Sanders to hit a ground ball to third which Mueller fielded cleanly and stepped on third to end the inning. The Red Sox won the game 6-2 and in the post-game press conference Schilling was asked about the four errors behind him and in particular about the three that Mueller committed. Schilling responded, "Bill Mueller is such a great teammate....When he made that error in the sixth and Sanders ended up coming up as the tying run.....I bore down as hard on him as any batter all night......I knew that Billy would feel terrible if they ended up tying that game and I did not want him to feel that."

Curt Schilling cared about his teammates, not just as guys he played a game with, but he cared about them personally!

Men, baseball is a game of coming back from failure. Pitchers are going to give up hits, they're going to give up runs. Infielders are going to boot the ball, they're going to throw balls away, hitters are going to fail to execute. It's all a part of the game. When it happens, YOU be the guy who picks up that guy that has failed. YOU be the one to step up and make the next play or strike the next guy out or knock in the run. Pick each other up men, we're all in this together!

https://www.youtube.com/watch?v=lwjJg3vmM_Y

15. DEFINE YOURSELVES

HEAVE THE RING

This story was used following a malaise that overtook one of our teams following a state championship season. They had grown lethargic and appeared apathetic. It is a story to illustrate that they have to get and stay in the moment each and every day-Last season does not mean anything!

This motivator will require some theatrics on the part of the coach as well as two visual aids.

It can best be explained within the context of how it was used and then it will be clearly understood. It was in the year following a State Championship season. The team was lethargic and seemingly had lost their drive. They had been playing with an attitude that projected that they just had to show up, throw their gloves on the field and they'd win.

Coach gathered the team in left field for their pre-game meeting. He reached in his pocket and pulled out the State Championship ring. "You guys remember this right?" he asked. The sight of the ring induced smiles on the faces of the players who were on last year's team and piqued the interest of the new comers. "Take a look at it." He said and he passed it around and as it went from player to player he asked each player to read the year on it. As the ring was going around Coach reminisced about some of the great moments from the championship season.

When the ring found its way back to him he took it and slipped it his back pocket, replacing it with a bolt which he kept grasped in his hand as he continued. "Men" he began and he again asked the question, "What was the year on that ring?" Of course the response was last year, to which he responded. "We are not last year's team. We did not earn that ring, last year's team earned that ring. Whatever we take from this season will be what we earn. It will require a full commitment to excellence, a complete focused effort on every inning of every game and it has to start tonight. Last year is gone men, it means nothing to any of our opponents and it means nothing in terms of what we will do as a team this year. It is time to define ourselves men."

Coach then turned toward the left field fence and heaved the bolt over the wall saying, "and it starts tonight!" And he walked away.

There is a caveat with this story. The left field fence in our park borders the intercostal waterway and there was no possibility in "the ring" being found. It is important that you pick a spot where your "ring" cannot be discovered. The funny thing is that several players approached Coach at a later date and asked him if he ever found his "ring."

16. THE BLACKSMITH

STAYING FOCUSED

This is a practice story about the focus and purpose required in practice to reach the team objective. It's about dealing with the mental grind of the long season. It can also be used as a pregame story to keep focus throughout an entire game.

In the days of settling the American West; there was perhaps no more important man in the town than the Blacksmith. It was he who was the town's iron worker and perhaps the most important function within that was shoeing horses. The horse was as essential then as the automobile is today. A man and his family were lost without their horse.

When the blacksmith began his job and pulled his iron from the fire, he did so knowing that it would take 2,000 licks with his hammer to his anvil to complete the horse shoe. Two thousand times he would strike the flat and straight steel bar to achieve his desired result. No strike was more important than another. Lick number 22 was as important as lick number 555! The noble blacksmith knew in his pursuit of a shoe worthy of a noble horse that lick number 2,000 could not be reached without lick number one; and all the licks in between. It was a total, unified, concentrated effort to achieve the desired goal.

This team has to approach each and every day, each and every practice, each and every at bat, bullpen, ground ball, fly ball with the mentality of a blacksmith! With the unyielding desire to focus to the task at hand each and every day, one lick at a time. Then and only then can we progress to our desired goal.

Be blacksmiths men. Be that noble blacksmith.

17. BURN THE BOATS

NO TURNING BACK

This is a story to be used to challenge a player and or a team to take the necessary steps to turn the corner; to forego old habits and embrace what it will take to commit to be the very best that they can be.

In February of 1519, Hernando Cortez set sail from Cuba to the Yucatan Peninsula in command of 11 ships, with 500 soldiers, 100 sailors and 16 horses. His quest was for a treasure the likes of which the world had never seen. As the natural perils of the ocean journey began to unfold there were those among the crew who began to doubt the mission. They groused about the difficulties encountered and discontent began to spread. Upon landing in Mexico, Cortez knew he had a problem on his hands, he knew he was in danger of a mutiny and losing his crew. He knew something dramatic had to take place to save his mission, to save his crew and indeed save himself.

The morning they were to begin their quest for the previously unreachable treasure, he gathered his men. " Men" he said, "today we begin a quest for a treasure that for six centuries has been unattainable…We must fight like no warriors have ever fought….If we are leaving here, we will do so in THEIR boats." He then shouted the command, "Burn the Boats!!!" As he did so his men, stationed on the decks of his 11 ships, torched the boats.

This added new meaning to their mission, new energy to their quest and they rededicated themselves to that effort and they succeeded, garnering a treasure that all thought was impossible to attain.

Men, we have reached this level with dedication and hard work. It is now time for us to reexamine where we are as individual players and as a team. It is time to look deep inside ourselves and see what is needed to improve, to get to the next level. And what is it that is holding us back? It might be that we simply have not totally committed to our mission. It might be an old habit that we are comfortable with that is impeding you. It might be that you are having difficulty recognizing or accepting your weaknesses. It is time to burn those boats gentlemen. It is time to look inside and recommit, to rededicate yourselves to making it to the next level!

18. WHOVILLE

CREATING EXPECTATIONS

This is a seasonal theme and can be used after your team from the previous year has lost some exceptional talent, thus lowering expectations for the coming year.

It is safe to say that every player at every level in every sport has at some point in time read, or at least heard of Dr. Seuss. The celebrated author is loved by children and adults for his poignant stories with a message and a moral that are often told in rhyme.

Whoville is a fictional place Dr. Seuss created in two of his books; *Horton Hears a Who* and *How the Grinch Stole Christmas*. It is the Grinch version we use here.

In the Grinch, Whoville is a small town located in a snowflake. The Grinch is a grouchy cave-dwelling curmudgeon whose heart is two sizes too small. He lives in his cave in a mountain above Whoville. One Christmas he is just so annoyed by the Christmas songs and good cheer coming from Whoville he decides to put an end to it by stealing all their trees, presents, and food. Disguising himself as Santa Claus and his dog Max as a reindeer, he sneaks into Whoville one night and successfully steals manifestations of Christmas taking from every house: every present, every tree, every decoration, and every morsel of food. He spends all night struggling back to the top of his mountain with his overflowing sleigh.

He reaches the top of Mount Crumpit and as he is preparing to dump everything into the abyss; he hears Christmas songs coming from Whoville below. Perplexed, he hesitates and wonders how it is that they can be so happy and the realization comes to him that Christmas is more than all the trappings. "Maybe Christmas means more" he thinks to himself, and when he does, his heart grows to three times its size. He returns everything to the people of Whoville and joins them in their Christmas celebration.

As we began our workouts, we talked to the team about Dr. Zeuss and *Whoville*. Our message was clear.

Gentlemen; last year we graduated some key players from our team. These players were part of two state championship teams and another visit to the Final Four. This off season our coaches were asked a lot of questions about who would replace this guy, who would replace that guy? There are a lot of Grinchs around the league who think our heart is not big enough; they think we've lost too much, they think we're rebuilding. Many of our own fans don't think we have what it takes to maintain the level of success we have recently enjoyed.

Men that's because they do not know who we are! We are Whoville. We are a team that has talent, that knows how to play the game and above all we have heart. We will spend the year showing all of them, one pitch at a time, one inning at a time, one groundball at a time, one at bat at a time, all of them will come to know OUR HEART, all will come to know who we are, WE ARE WHOVILLE!

Visual aids were added to our field for the year as signs were hung in the outfield reading simply "Whoville Population 56" which included all members of our varsity and JV squads, and coaches. Initials, "WDWD" ("Who Dat We Dat"), were placed on the back of our caps the meaning which was known only to us. The entire year was spent defining Whoville, first to ourselves and then to everyone else!

This was adopted by our team during summer workouts six months before the season began. It followed a third straight trip to the State Final Four in which two resulted in back to back State Championships.

That season resulted in a fourth straight visit to the Final Four and a third State Championship in four years, a fourth in eight years and a ranking of third in the nation in the final Baseball America prep poll.

Whoville is engraved on their rings!

19. SHOOT ME

WAKE-UP! THERE'S A TARGET ON YOUR BACK!
A STORY FOR THE TRANSITION

This is a motivational story told during a season in which our team became the hunted. It was one of those stories which, after the telling, became a theme for the remainder of the season that was adopted by the team. These are, more often than not, the most effective motivators of all; those nuggets that the team chooses to latch on to and which they use to define themselves! This story will require some drama and a visual aid.

The team had been an "up and coming team" as the previous year we had registered some unexpected wins. We had been sneaking up on people and winning games that raised eyebrows around the district and the area. The subsequent season we stumbled out of the gate with a 6-7 record and we were really floundering. It was clear that we were no longer going to sneak up on people and the players could not seem to grasp that we were now the hunted.

So one day at practice, one of the coaches was "missing." As the team was warming up, the "missing" coach climbed a ladder he had placed behind the outfield wall. He stood on the top of the wall and starting yelling "Shoot me, Shoot me" as he paced back and forth across the top of the wall. He was wearing a camo hunting hat on which he painted in florescent orange the words "shoot me." The players were startled at the "crazy guy" but as they recognized that it was coach, they then became intrigued.

Coach came down from the wall as the players were huddled up. Coach went over to the dugout and brought a bag back to the huddle. In the bag was 20 camo hats with the words "Shoot Me" painted on in the same fluorescent orange. "Here you go fellas" coach said as he gave each one of them a cap. This is the way we're playing so we might as well just have it out there. We are wandering around in an open field and letting ourselves get picked off. We need to change the way we are doing things, we need to realize that we are now in a position where we are going to see everybody's best pitcher; we are going to get everybody's best effort! It's time to change our approach men or we will be shot.

From that day on, the players hung one of those caps in the dug-out. We won 11 of our next 12 games and captured a district championship. In the regional final we defeated the number one ranked team in the state.

The hunted responded!!!

20. RESTORE RESPECT

PUTTING YOUR PROGRAM BACK ON LINE FOLLOWING
A TOUGH PREVIOUS YEAR

*This is a theme to use when you have suffered a poor season
after one or more successful ones. This is a true story.*

Following our first State Championship in 2007, we were no longer a
team that was going to sneak up on anybody. The target was now in
full view and it was on our backs. We graduated 11 seniors that year
and the following season had a record just above .500. A year later we
endured our worst season on the field going 9-17.

A few coaches were at our district meeting and the discussion was
taking place to decide where the District Tournament should take
place. The coach of one of our arch rivals stated, "Keep the tournament in Venice, they have the best facility." Another coach disagreed
stating, "Why would we want to give them a home field edge?" To
which came the response, "They are not the threat they once were."

We no longer snuck up on anyone and we provoked no fear in our
opponents; our program was back at square one!

At the outset we related that very story and challenged our seniors
to lead the charge in "Restoring Respect." We had a yellow patch with
the railroad crossing R/R sewn on the back of our game caps and
hammered that theme all season long! The seniors stepped up and
with the assistance of some very talented underclassmen, including
two freshmen starters, the team finished 19-10. And they won the
District Championship, at home.

21. OUR CHIPS, OUR CHAIR, OUR HOUSE

NOT IN OUR HOUSE

This story can be used following a home loss that did not seem to bother the team as much as it should have. The site of visiting players celebrating a big win on their field did not leave them frustrated or angry. The team seemed to simply accept it as part of a natural course of events.

Choose a player on your team with whom to begin this conversation. It would be helpful if this player's dad is known to be somewhat of a tough man. The conversation could go something like this:

Coach: Jimmy what's your dad do for a living?

Jimmy: He's a plumber sir.

Coach: A plumber huh, so it is fair to say that he physically works hard long days.

Jimmy: Yes sir.

Coach: I assume dad has a favorite chair.

Jimmy: Yes he does.

Coach: Of course, all dad's do. So let's suppose that dad comes home from work one day and sitting in his favorite chair is some guy. Some guy he didn't know. He has an open bag of chips that he's snacking on, feet are up and he's watching the news. **IN DADS CHAIR!** What do you think would happen?

This conversation will trigger a visceral response and will be entertaining as various players will add into the conversation what would happen in their house.

Men, those guys came into our house the other night. They didn't even knock! They kicked in the door, tore open the cupboards, grabbed a drink, **SAT IN YOUR CHAIR,** did whatever they came to do and left! Left this place a mess and the worst part is, it didn't even seem to bother you!

You have got to understand that every time you see those guys in that other dugout they are here to: kick in **YOUR** door, open up **YOUR** cupboards, grab a bag of **YOUR** chips, pull open **YOUR** refrigerator, grab **YOUR** cold drink, plop down in **YOUR** chair, in **YOUR** living room, put their feet up and watch **YOUR** TV. Gentlemen that is unacceptable to any of us! It is **OUR** chips, **OUR** chair and **OUR** house….Tonight we make them wish they never stopped by!

This was very effective used late in one season following a tough loss at home. It became a rallying cry that the players themselves adopted through the end of the season. From that point on a game did not go by that a reference to this was not used. Obviously the home reference was always present however this particular team used it on the road as well, with phrases such as, "let's get us some chips tonight", or "let's go sit in their chair." In fact it became such a part of their make-up that it was engraved on the inside of their State Championship rings! Our chips, our chair, our house!

22. SET SAIL FOR THE MOON

SETTING HIGH EXPECTATIONS.

This story can be used as a team theme for the season. It must be a year when you are ready to challenge your team to think big. You can wrap your year around the high objectives set and you can refer back to the failures of the space program (a few are contained in this book) when your season hits bumps. It can also be used in a pregame setting. There are two endings here depending upon which you choose.

On May 25, 1961 in a speech before Congress, John F Kennedy set America's sights for the moon. It was exactly 16 days after Mercury astronaut Alan Sheppard, had completed NASA's first manned mission; a modest 15 minute 22 second sub-orbital flight. Sixteen months later, he stood before 40,000 people on a sweltering September day at Rice University in Houston Texas and he uttered his country's clarion call challenging America and Americans to rally to a mission which man had never before embarked upon.

He outlined that mission and set America's, indeed Mankind's course.

"If I were to say, my fellow citizens, that we shall send to the moon, 240,000 miles away from the control station in Houston, a giant rocket more than 300 feet tall, the length of this football field, made of new metal alloys, some of which have not yet been invented, capable of standing heat and stresses several times more than have ever been experienced, fitted together with a precision better than the finest watch, carrying all the equipment needed for propulsion, guidance, control, communications, food and survival, on an untried mission, to an unknown celestial body, and then return it safely to earth, re-entering the atmosphere at speeds of over 25,000 miles per hour, causing heat about half that of the temperature of the sun--almost as hot as it is here today--and do all this, and do it right, and do it first before this decade is out--then we must be bold."

Many doubted the soundness of this goal, they doubted America's ability to accept this challenge and meet the objective. For at this time the United States had succeeded in but four manned spaceflights, two sub-orbital. Astronauts John Glenn (3 orbits) and Wally Shirra (6 orbits) were the only Americans to have orbited the earth. Meanwhile the Soviets were clearly the leaders in the space race.

Recognizing the fears, the trepidation, the challenge of his goal the president was undaunted and threw down the gauntlet.

"We choose to go to the moon. We choose to go to the moon in this decade and do the other things, not because they are easy, but because they are hard, because that goal will serve to organize and measure the best of our energies and skills, because that challenge is one that we are willing to accept, one we are unwilling to postpone, and one which we intend to win."

On July 20th 1969, United States astronaut Neil Armstrong became the first man to walk on the moon. President John F Kennedy was not alive to witness this historic event having been assassinated in November of 1963.

It took a total of 29 space flights before Armstrong landed The Eagle on the moon. Three Americans died in the effort and there were several more near misses including Armstrong himself who nearly tumbled into space aboard a Gemini craft.

Through it all, America and Americans prevailed. Twelve men have walked on the moon and there are six American flags in six different moon locations. All started with the acceptance of a challenge. A challenge to do better, a challenge to rise to the best within us, a challenge to refuse to let anything stand in the way of our goal, of our objective. And all accomplished by not just the astronauts but the NASA support at mission control numbering in the hundreds.

Preseason setting:

It was a monstrous goal and in the eyes of many, impossible to achieve. We have set our own high goals for this season. It will take belief in our ability to achieve it and an enormous amount of hard work! JFK set the challenge all those years ago and today I set before you this challenge; "Let's win it all."

Pregame setting:

Tonight will require the very best that is within you as individuals and within us not only as individuals but as a team. Tonight requires all the energy that you can muster whether you are on the field or in the dugout. We need each of us to be ready, to be focused, to be undaunted by the task before us!!!!

Go out tonight and take it!!!

https://www.youtube.com/watch?v=kwFvJog2dMw

23. SELF EVALUATE

DON'T STOP WORKING TO IMPROVE
WHEN YOU ARE ON TOP.

This is a practice story on self-evaluation to keep your team from being lulled into complacency when all is going well. A story to help them keep focus and understand that dedication, effort and commitment must be maintained.

When a season is going exceptionally well, when all things are clicking and the team is enjoying tremendous success; believe it or not, there is danger looming. We learned this lesson one year after setting a school record of 16 straight wins and also was ranked number one in the state. We ended the season with nine losses and did not make it into the District Playoffs. WE DID NOT DO ENOUGH SELF EVALUATING! And when things got tough, panic set in.

History and sports are filled with stories of seemingly invincible teams collapsing and enormously successful companies going under.

In 1996, PGA great Greg Norman carried a six-shot lead into the Masters final day to end up losing by five strokes. The 1993 AFC Wildcard game found the Houston Oilers leading the Buffalo Bills 35-3 at halftime, only to lose 41-38 in overtime. French golfer Jean Van De Velde stood on the 18th tee at Carnoustie in 1999 with a three-shot lead, needing only a double bogey to win the British Open on a hole he had birdied twice during the tournament. He shot a seven and was virtually never heard from again. And even the mighty New York Yankees fell victim in 2004, leading the Red Sox 3-0 in the ALCS they become the first team in baseball history to lose a 3-0 lead, in a seven game series, and fall.

These collapses are not simply confined to the playing fields. It happens in business as well. Nobody captured the home movie and game market like Blockbuster video. Begun as a single store in 1980, it peaked in 2004 with 60,000 employees and 9,000 stores. Outgunned by Netflix and Red Box, they filed for bankruptcy in 2010 and the following year the company was bought at auction by the Dish Network.

Perhaps the most famous name in photography is Kodak. Founded by George Eastman in 1892, the Eastman Kodak Company was a veritable giant for a century on the American business scene. However, they failed to recognize and adjust to the digital photography technology and in 2012, 120 years after its founding, they filed for bankruptcy!

Gentlemen, each of these stories has a common thread and that thread is a failure to self-evaluate. A failure to recognize that things will not always go your way simply because they have in the past or are doing so now. If we do not recognize that we must maintain a focus, and work hard, we will not be prepared when things go wrong and panic will ensue. Failure thrives in panic!

No matter how well we are playing, no matter how many breaks we are getting, we know that we must stay focused and continue to work to get better. And we are prepared for the adversity so when it arrives WE WILL NOT PANIC! We will handle it!

24. TAKING DOWN THE BULLY

RUFUS MAYNARD

This is a totally fictional, yet very effective, story to use when you are taking on that very good team such as a perennial powerhouse from outside the area. The kind of team that chirps a lot, argues with umpires, has the rowdy fans, runs up the score and overall does not show much of a respect for the game. It would not hurt that the team is not particularly well-liked or that you may be an underdog in the contest.

This story has two props, an open pad lock and a wooden stick.

This is the story of two 13 year old boys. The first one's name is Rufus Maynard. Rufus was a very big kid hitting 6 feet 4 inches in height and he weighed in at 188 lbs. A full head of red hair he already had started to shave and he had a terrible case of acne. Both his parents worked at night and always stopped in the local bar for breakfast. Rufus got himself off to school in the morning and by the time he got home his folks were in bed. Unchecked, he was virtually raising himself and his favorite school activity was to bully kids. He had three favorite bullying activities. One was the simple shake down in which he would threatened his fellow students until they handed over their lunch money. The second was the simple beat up which was exactly what it sounds like; he would target a kid and simply beat him up on the playground. The third one was the wedgie. He did one, two, or all three of them virtually every day.

Johnathan Needham was 5 foot 1 inch tall and weighed 92 lbs. A quiet nerdy kid, he kept to himself, bothered no one and he played the clarinet in the school band. He was often the target for Rufus' antics.

It all changed in a day! And it was a day that Johnathan was not even the target, but it was a day Johnathan had planned for a while.

After watching Rufus have a particularly lucrative shakedown day, Johnathan mustered all that was in him and screamed out, "Rufus, it stops today!" The playground activity stopped as all eyes turned to Johnathan. Rufus was on the other side of the playground and when he heard Johnathan, he stood up and started to laugh. "Everybody out" Johnathan yelled and all the kids made their way out the gate. Rufus just watched amused. When the last kid left through the gate, Johnathan reached into his pocket, pulled out the lock and locked the gate! (Here's where coach does the same.)

Just Rufus and Johnathan were inside and Johnathan turned to Rufus who was now walking toward him, 'What are you gonna do about it nerd ball?" Rufus was yelling as the two made their way to the center of the field. Now facing each other Rufus chided him again. "What's puny little Johnathan gonna do, huh?" And he began to shake his finger in Johnathan's face. "Not very smart Johnathan, especially for a nerd." Johnathan grabbed Rufus' finger and snapped it! (Coach snaps the stick in two) Rufus let out a yell and doubled over at which point Johnathan gave Rufus a wedgie so big he tied his shorts under his neck like a bow tie, turned, unlocked the gate and left. Rufus ran home crying to the astonishment of everyone watching.

Gentlemen, these guys have been bullying people all year. They run their mouths, they show no respect to any opponent, and they run up scores and berate teams when they do. They make a mockery of the game! It ends tonight men! Tonight we lock the gate and snap the finger off of Rufus Maynard and send him home crying!

25. NO WEAK LINKS

HOW HARD IS EVERYONE WORKING?

This is a locker room story that will require visual aids, specifically, three lengths of chain approximately three feet long. It is a story which will illustrate commitment to the team, its goals and what it will take to achieve them. This story can be told at practice or in the locker room and should be used at the start of the season.

The story begins with Coach talking about the team; the commitment required of each player to work hard, be the best they can be and strive toward the stated goal as individuals and as a team. Incorporated within is the phrase "we do not want any weak links here." At this point Coach holds up the chain and says simply "show me the weak link." Of course there is no identifiable weak link. They all look the same, sturdy and strong. You could even pass the link around and have the players hold it, inspect it. As they are passing it around Coach says; "It is weak links that will cause a team to fail." When the chain gets back to the coach, he takes out a cutter and cuts it in half. He then secures a large paper clip and rejoins the severed pieces, holding it up before the group. When held up to the group everyone will obviously see where this chain will fail. Have a player grab the other end of the chain and pull. The paper clip will give and the chain will be broken. Holding both pieces up Coach says; "That link must be replaced, rehabilitated or removed!" Continuing he says, "However that weak link is not the worst kind, as it is easily identified and can be dealt with."

At this time Coach pulls out another piece of chain, only the players do not know that a hack saw has been cut through a random link (half the link completely through and the other half significantly through) creating a far less conspicuous weak link. Holding it up, there is no clearly identifiable spot on the chain that appears weak. Coach may say, "This chain looks strong, capable and ready to handle its job." Then Coach lays the chain on the floor, steps on it and pulls until the link gives and breaks. Lifting the chain from the floor it is shown to the players.

"Looked strong, looked ready, and appeared perfect"!

Only you know how hard you are working, only you know if you are going through the motions, only you know if you are on board, are committed, are dedicating yourself completely to the team, to the goal," NO WEAK LINKS !!!

To rededicate the team to the task at hand, pull out a third chain and with a sharpie have each player write their number on a link. You then may use the link at appropriate times throughout the season as a way of rededicating them all to the effort!

26. PEARL HARBOR

STAY PREPARED

"To be prepared is half the victory." —*Miguel Cervantes*

A story about staying focused and being prepared at all times. Take no team for granted, take no win for granted, and take NOTHING for granted.

On December 7, 1941, it was a beautiful Sunday morning on the Island of Oahu, Hawaii. The world was at war but to the inhabitants of the US Military Installation that war was far, far away. It was raging in China where the Japanese war machine was on the march and it was raging in Europe where the Nazi war machine was also on the march. But the paradise islands of Hawaii, particularly Oahu, seemed impervious to an attack. The belief was that the water was too shallow for a sub attack and the simple vastness of the Pacific would prevent an air attack.

The day before, the United States intercepted Japanese messages which told them that an attack appeared imminent. However, the best guess was that it would take place in Southeast Asia, perhaps at the American military base in Thailand. Meanwhile six Japanese carriers with 483 planes on board were preparing for attack. At 6am, the first 183 planes departed their carriers; they were 230 miles from Oahu, their target, the United States fleet anchored at Pearl Harbor. At 7:02am, two US Army radar operators on Oahu's north shore detected an air attack and notified a junior officer. The warning was disregarded, dismissed as the expected arrival of American P-17's expected from the west coast. Less than 15 minutes later, an additional 167 planes left the decks of Japanese carriers; the success of their sneak attack, now assured.

Japanese bombers dropped their first bombs at 7:53am, and the last one an hour and fifty- two minutes later. This left 2,403 Americans dead, and 1,178 wounded; 1,104 of the deaths were crewmen of the USS Arizona who to this day still lay resting in her hull at the bottom of Pearl Harbor. Five battleships were sunk, three damaged, and 188 aircraft were lost. The planes were lined up on the airstrip wing tip to wing tip. They were sitting ducks.

Admiral Husband E. Kimmel, the commander of the Pacific fleet and Army Lt. General Walter C Short were both relieved of their command. Patriots both, it was their responsibility to keep the men, keep the base prepared. They were lulled to sleep and paid a dear price.

Gentlemen, we are not engaged in war, lives are not at stake, but nonetheless we can learn from the tragic error of Pearl Harbor. It is a simple lesson but it can be difficult to prevent. Never be lulled by an opponent. Never make the mistake of disrespecting your opposition. Remember just how difficult it is to stay focused and just how diligent you must be, as an individual and as a team, to keep your edge, and to stay prepared. It is unpreparedness that leads to over-confidence and it is overconfidence which slays giants!

DO NOT BE LULLED INTO DEFEAT by taking one small detail for granted!

https://www.youtube.com/watch?v=bxIsVYdB0lA

CHAPTER TWO

THE MIND OF THE COMPETITOR

27. THE BED BY THE WINDOW

YOU CHOOSE YOUR ATTITUDE

This is a story to use when you have players lack of playing time beginning to effect the team in a negative way. It will help to refocus their thoughts on team and not themselves.

Two seriously ill men occupied the same hospital room. One man was by the window while the other had to remain flat on his back and saw nothing but the ceiling above him. The men spoke for hours on end as they told each other of their wives, their families, their homes, careers, vacations. They exchanged stories of their military service and in fact grew quite close in a short period of time.

Every afternoon the man by the window would look out and give a detailed description of what he saw to his friend in the next bed. The man came to live each day for that time when his world would be broadened and brought to life by the activity, the color and the beauty of the outside world. His friend told him of a park with a lovely pond in its midst. Ducks and swans swam among children sailing model boats in the shallow waters. Lovers walked arm and arm amidst an array of flowers of all colors and grand old trees reached for the sky. Beyond it all was the beautiful view of the city skyline. The meticulous exquisite details brought the outside world to life in the mind's eye of the man whose eyes saw only the ceiling.

As the weeks passed the man began to envy his friend by the window and one night he fell asleep with thoughts of seeing the outside world for himself.

Morning came and he was awakened by the commotion in the room as the nurse had discovered the lifeless body of the man by the window. She informed the man of the death of his roommate. "I know how close you were" she said, "I'm very sorry." He only nodded as she closed the curtain so they could remove his lifeless friend.

After his friend was moved, the nurse returned telling the man they were putting him by the window, "the sunlight will do you good" she said and she moved his bed across the room and left him alone. Still flat on his back, he could not quite see out the window but he was determined and although he was supposed to remain flat he began to struggle to lift himself to see outside. Slowly, painfully he struggled to prop himself up on his elbow. He struggled and fell but was determined that he would have the joy of seeing what was outside that window for himself. He pushed again and finally he raised his head high enough and looked out the window. Staring back at him was the blank wall of the building next door!

Gentlemen, we can learn from both of these men.

How many of you wish you had that bed by the window? In fact who among you is so disappointed that your selfish pursuits now consume you? You have to see the big picture! You may not be playing every day, you may not like the coach, or one of your teammates, you may not be playing as well as you want, you may feel you are not doing what you should be doing or playing where and when you should be playing.

And if you are that man by the window; if you are a starter, help the backup players, put them first, for whichever role you are now in, you are a needed part of this team! You are part of something that is bigger than you and only YOU have the power to make this a positive, joyful experience or a negative one. Your attitude today will decide how you will look back on this experience 10 years from now.

The pursuit of happiness is a choice men….It is a positive attitude we consciously choose to express!

28. DIAMONDS-HEAT AND PRESSURE

HOW WILL YOU RESPOND? THIS IS A QUICK LITTLE
PREGAME STORY BEFORE A BIG GAME.

There are no stones on the planet more valued than diamonds. They symbolize so much within our culture: excellence, value and commitment. They are sought after and they are cherished.

Where do they come from and how do they get here? First, understand they are crystals that form under crushing pressure and intense heat. The pressure which produces them would be equivalent to approximately 4000 grown men standing on your foot. This combined with temperatures of roughly 2700 degrees Fahrenheit will ultimately give us the diamond in all its splendor and beauty.

All this takes place between 87 and 125 miles deep in the bowels of the earth.

Gentlemen, this game that you play on, a diamond will produce crushing pressure and intense heat. It may find you looking for breath. The heat of fierce competition will wilt many! You must go deep inside you and find the tools within to embrace the pressure, to welcome the heat! It is in you!

Tonight it is all on the line, the pressure you feel is a source of energy, and the heat is your friend. We love the heat, we love the pressure. We embrace them both for it is what makes us great! This night, this games is yours. Tonight we become the brightest diamond! Go out there and get it.

29. THE MULE IN THE WELL

GETTING BACK UP AFTER A FALL.

"That which does not kill me, only makes me stronger."
Friedrich Nietzsche

This is a practice story to use before the season begins or when your team has hit some early bumps. It could be used pregame as well.

A parable is told of a farmer who owned an old mule. The mule fell into the farmer's dry well. The farmer heard the mule "braying" or whatever mules do when they fall into dry wells. After carefully assessing the situation, the farmer sympathized with the mule, but decided that neither the mule nor the dry well was worth the trouble of saving. Instead, he called his neighbors together and told them what had happened and enlisted them to help haul dirt to bury the old mule in the well to put him out of his misery.

Initially, as the dirt landed on him, the old mule panicked. But as the farmer and his neighbors continued shoveling the dirt upon his back, a thought suddenly struck him. Every time a shovel load of dirt landed on his back, he could SHAKE IT OFF AND STEP UP! This he did, shovel full after shovel full. "Shake it off and step up...shake it off and stand up...shake it off and stand up!" he repeated to encourage himself. No matter how painful the dirt was when it hit his back, or distressing the situation seemed, the old mule fought "panic" and just kept on SHAKING IT OFF AND STEPPING UP!

It wasn't long before the old mule, battered and exhausted, STEPPED TRIUMPHANTLY OVER THE WALL OF THAT WELL! The situation that seemed at first like it would bury him, actually blessed him, all because of the manner in which he handled his adversity.

Every baseball season will present adversity, will present challenges and obstacles. We will face each one of them, refuse to give in to panic, to bitterness, to self-pity. The tough times we will shake off and we will step up. Some individuals, some teams are buried by adversity, not us! For that which does not kill us, will only make us stronger.

http://achievebalance.com/spirit/buried.htm

30. BELIEVE IN YOURSELF.

DOUG FLUTIE..TOO SMALL FOR GREATNESS?

This is a story of singularity of purpose, determination and belief in oneself. It can be used with an individual player who is having trouble with confidence and belief in themselves and it can be adapted to a team situation where an opponent is clearly physically bigger and stronger.

He was born in Maryland in 1962, and he was 14 years old when his family moved to Natick, Massachusetts where the legend that would come to be known as Doug Flutie took hold. You're too small Flutie often heard when it came to athletic endeavors, just too small. His response to that was to become an All-League high school performer in football, basketball and baseball.

All set to go to the University of New Hampshire, Boston College offered him their last scholarship in 1981. However his size was considered a hindrance to playing quarterback and many thought he was better suited to be a defensive back. His freshman year he was the team's number five quarterback.

In a span of six weeks he won the starting job. SIX WEEKS!!!!

The country's ninth ranked passer as a freshman; in his sophomore year he led BC to their first bowl game in 40 years. He threw for 520 yards against the soon to be National Champions Penn State and although they lost to Bo Jackson's Auburn Tigers in the Tangerine Bowl, Flutie was the game's MVP! In his junior year he became one of the nation's elite players finishing third in the Heisman Trophy balloting and being named a second team All American. It was in his senior year that the legend of Doug Flutie was cemented and the "Flutie Effect" became a phrase in the lexicon of college sports which is still used today.

In 1984, the legend of Doug Flutie was cemented into the annals of American sports! Named a consensus All American, he also won; the Heisman Trophy, the Walter Camp Player of the Year Award, the Maxwell Player of the Year Award, and the Davey O'Brien Award as the NCAA quarterback of the year. He was immortalized by the "Miracle in Miami" in a game which in reality was a microcosm of his entire football career at every level.

Following Flutie's incredible 1984 season Boston College led to a significant increase in applicants the following year; a phenomenon which came to be known as the Flutie Effect.

The kid who was simply too small went on to a 20 year career in professional football; 14 years in the NFL and six in the Canadian Football League. A pro bowler with the Buffalo Bills in 1998, Doug Flutie left the Canadian Football League the all-time leader with 41,355 yards passing and he still holds the record for touchdown passes in a season with 48 in 1994 with the Calgary Stampeders.

A member of the College Football Hall of Fame and the Canadian Football Hall of Fame, Doug Flutie, the kid who was too small, in 2006 was voted the greatest player in the history of the Canadian Football League!

The 5' 9" 175 lb. too small quarterback had proven to the world that you are only as small as you think you are! Believing it can happen is 90% of achieving!

Doug Flutie

https://www.youtube.com/watch?v=PoCOwlPi6yg

Miracle in Miami

https://www.youtube.com/watch?v=ZeExa2R2nf0

31. BANGITY BANG—BELIEVE

BE TOUGHER THAN YOUR OPPONENT.

This is a story of belief in every player's ability to succeed and therefore the ultimate success of the team. It will be most effective before a game.

This is a story about a young man who had failed at virtually everything he had attempted to do. He dropped out of high school the day he turned 16. He knocked around at some odd jobs here and there for a couple of years and after being laid off, again, he decided he would do something to make a positive difference in his life!

He scoured the newspapers and he found an ad looking for volunteers to fight a war of liberation in a third world country. Intrigued by this idea, he was overcome with a sense of purpose. The next morning he signed up and within a week he was on his way! After nine weeks of extensive physical training, he was told by the commander to get a good night's rest, "for tomorrow we go into battle."

The commander returned to his office leaving the young man dumbfounded. After sitting a bit, the young soldier mustered the courage to knock on the commander's door. "Come in" he hears behind the door and he slowly opened it. "Can I talk with you sir?" "Sure soldier, what's your problem?" "Sir" he said, "I don't have a gun." "Course not" the commander responded, "of course not." "Well what am I supposed to do?" "Believe" came the response. "Believe what sir?" The commander stood up and looked the young man in the eyes and said, "Soldier you must believe that all you need do is point your finger at the enemy and scream "bangity bang, bangity bang! And you will kill him dead in his tracks." Lost in a sea of incredulity he hears the commander, "Anything else soldier?" "No sir" he heard himself grumble. 'Dismissed."

The next day the company moved out it was not long before they were taking fire. Paralyzed with fear, the young soldier hid in the rear, never engaging in the battle. That night, the commander ordered him to his tent and told the young soldier he knew he had hid from battle and he wanted to know why! "Bangity bang sir….really?" "Listen son" the commander said, "in your whole life you have never believed in anything, you must believe in something son, you must believe in this system for it to succeed, for you to succeed, you're either in or you're out!"

When the company moved out in the morning, the soldier was with them. Terrified he encountered his first action. Summoning all the courage he could muster, he pointed his finger and screamed "Bangity bang, bangity bang" and to his astonishment the enemy fell around him.

He became one of the finest fighting men this army had ever seen. He was brave, courageous and bold and all others looked to him! And then the day came. He was in battle and firing "Bangity bang, bangity bang" yet the enemy kept coming. "Bangity bang, bangity bang." Still advancing the enemy rolled him over, wounding him fatally. As he lay dying on the battlefield he was wondering what had gone wrong and then he heard the advancing enemy muttering something. He listened closer and he heard their words, "Tankity tank, tankity tank they were saying as they proceeded forward.

If you believe gentlemen you will prevail, you will overcome. Take the field tonight believing in yourselves, in each other, in your coaches, in your team and in our purpose! Believe BIG! BELIEVE we can prevail and we will!!!

32. STAYING THE COURSE

NED GARVER-NEVER STOP COMPETING

This is a practice story to tell your team when your season is going bad and there appears to be no hope. It is a story about a player who chose to simply compete.

The game of baseball is the most difficult to play and nothing is more difficult than to maintain your competitive edge and focus when the team is going poorly. It is hard to match the fun and enjoyment of playing on a team that is winning. When all is going well, everybody wants to be at the ball park. Everybody can't wait to get to practice. Conversely, when a team is losing, the season can be interminable and feels like it will never end. It is at these times that baseball will test you to your physical and mental limits! It will challenge you in ways you never dreamed possible. It will expose your character.

There may have never been a player to answer that particular challenge better than Ned Franklin Garver. Ned Garver signed with the St. Louis Browns (they became the Baltimore Orioles in 1954) in 1944. He made his major league debut in 1948 but it was in 1951 that he did something that no other pitcher had ever done before and none has done since!

In 1951 Garver was the Browns' opening day starter and he gave up six runs in 1 2/3 innings as the White Sox thumped St. Louis 17-3. He won his next three games, all coming after a Browns loss and as the season progressed, Ned Garver emerged as a true ace. While the Browns were plummeting deeper and deeper into the abyss of the season, Garver kept competing.

St Louis hit last place on May 11th, 10 ½ games out. They flipped back and forth between seventh and eighth place (there were only eight teams in each league) until they entered the cellar to stay on

June 20th, 19 ½ games back. The plummet continued: 29 games out August 1st, 41 back on September 1st and on the next to last game of the year on September 29th, they reached a season low 46 games back with an 8-3 loss to the White Sox.

Meanwhile Garver took the ball every fourth day and on occasion he came out of the bullpen. He won 16 games after a Brown's loss and he led the league with 24 complete games. On September 7th he won his 16th game, a complete game 4-2 win against the Indians. He then ran off four more complete games winning three of them with two of them lasting 10 innings. He was now 19-12 and there was one game left to go. He took the ball hurling his sixth straight complete game and beating the White Sox 9-5 for his 20th win of the season!

The Browns finished the season 52-102 and 46 games behind the first place New York Yankees. Ned Garver became the first, last and only pitcher to date to win 20 games for a team that lost 100 or more games in a season.

Gentlemen, Ned Garver had one motivation during a season when his team was going nowhere- to compete. We have struggled this season, we have not clicked, but if each of you go out tonight with the goal to just compete, give every at bat, every pitch, every defensive play which comes your way your very best effort; you will be amazed at what is possible. Let's turn this around tonight!!!

33. OVERCOMING MENTAL BARRIERS

ROGER BANNISTER AND THE FOUR MINUTE MILE

This is a story about breaking through mental barriers and can be used in a practice situation speaking about the role the mind plays in competition, or it can be used before a game when you want to challenge your team to get to the next level.

Roger Bannister was a British med student who ran as an amateur. His event was the mile run. Long before the days of the commercialization (professionalization) of sports, the arena of track and field was purely an amateur endeavor with the Olympics as the ultimate goal of all who participated.

The twenty-five year old medical student was among the greatest milers in the world and as he trained for the 1952 Olympics in Helsinki; he not only was the favorite to win the Gold Medal, but many believed he would break the world record of 4:01 and some even thought he would become the first human to run the mile in under four minutes!

There was a mystique surrounding the barrier of the sub four minute mile. An underlying undertone among the general public that it was a physical impossibility and dangerous. Some even suggested that the human body was simply incapable of such a feat and the heart might even explode!

In the 1952 Olympics, Bannister finished fourth in the mile, not even receiving a medal. Despite the fact that he had set a new British record in the 1500 meter race, his Olympic effort of 1952 was considered a failure by most, including Bannister himself. For two months following the games, he gave serious consideration to giving up running. However, after contemplating retirement he decided instead to set a new goal-he set his sights on running a sub four minute mile!

Bannister returned to the track but his studies required a lot of his time and he was unable to give his running the time it needed. Despite this, he did run his personal best 4:02 mile on June 27th 1953. He knew then that the sub four minute mile was within reach.

He set his sights for May 6, 1954 in a race at the Iffley Road Track at Oxford University. Australian runner John Landy was also closing in on a sub four minute mile and this spurred Bannister on.

The day dawned rainy and windy and as Bannister made his morning hospital rounds doubt creeped in, for he felt that the weather conditions would have to be perfect for him to accomplish his seemingly impossible goal. On the afternoon train from London to Oxford he ran into Franz Stampfl, the coach of a teammate. Stampfl exhorted Bannister to take his shot, regardless of the weather telling him, "If you don't take this opportunity, you may never forgive yourself."

Roger Bannister arrived at the track, still undecided if he would make the concerted effort necessary to reach his goal. As he was warming up, he looked at the flag flying over St. John the Evangelist Church and said to himself; "if everyone in rainy and windy England waited for good weather before doing anything, nothing would ever be done." At that moment he went to two of his teammates and told them he was going all out to finish in under four minutes.

The race began and as the runners entered the final lap, Bannister was trailing. This was his custom as he had a kick at the finish that was as good as anyone had seen and this day would be no different. He passed all runners in front of him and as he came down the stretch a gust of wind pushed him sideways stealing the ever valuable fractions of a second! It was at that moment that the mind of Dr. Roger Bannister took over. He recalled the final seconds of the race; "I felt that the moment of a lifetime had come. There was no pain, only a great utility of movement and aim. The world seemed to stand still or did not exist, the only reality was the next two hundred yards of track under my feet."

He collapsed at the finish line nearly passing out when the announcer declared his time, 3:59.4 seconds! The impossible had become reality!!!

Bannister held this world record for exactly 46 days until his rival and friend John Landy broke it running a 3:58 mile; and just seven weeks later Bannister and Landy ran against each other and for the first time two runners ran it in under four minutes.

By the end of 1957, 16 runners had logged sub four minute miles and today that number has exceeded 1500. In 2001 the London Times named Roger Bannister's sub four minute mile the British Sporting Event of the 20th century!

Tonight remove those mental barriers which have held you back. Break through those and let yourself do something special, take that first huge step in redefining yourself as a player and open the door to your greatness!!! TONIGHT IS YOUR NIGHT!!!

http://www.encyclopedia.com/topic/Roger_Bannister.aspx

https://www.youtube.com/watch?v=wTXoTnp_5sl

34. COLONEL ROBERT HALL— VISUALIZE YOUR SUCCESS

COLONEL ROBERT HALL-THE POWER OF THE MIND

"Imagination is more important than knowledge"
—**Albert Einstein**

"Thought allied fearlessly to purpose becomes creative force,
he who knows this is ready to become something higher
and stronger than a mere bundle of wavering thoughts and
fluctuating sensations; he who does this has become the
conscious and intelligent wielder of his mental powers."
—**James Allen-British philosopher**

This is a practice story and it is one you might consider taking into a classroom and taking some time with. It is a bit technical with allusions to some scientific and philosophical components to it, but it will be worth the effort. Not many kids are aware of the role their mind can and will play in their success, not only as athletes but as people.

Today I want to throw another tool in your toolbox! The development of baseball skills is akin to re-creating yourself, and there is much to be said about the importance of the mind in this creation. The fact is, before any physical object can be created there must have first been imagined, a mental creation. It had to be visualized!!! The car you drive, the house you live in, and the computer you use for homework have all been created and visualized in someone's mind long before they appeared in their physical form.

The power of the mind and its role in sports competition is alluded to all the way back to the days of the early Greeks in the Olympic Games. However, it was in the 1930s in Germany and later in Russia, where it began to take on its modern form. It came to full fruition with the 1980 Russian Olympic teams. As they trained for the games, the teams were divided into four groups A, B, C and D. Group A trained in the traditional manner with 100% of the time devoted to physical training. Group B spent 75% of the time in physical training and 25% in training their minds. Group C was a 50/50 split and group D did 25% physical training and spent 75% of the time in mental training. When the games came to an end, it was Group D which won the most medals! As a result of this study, the 1988 Olympics found the United States team add a sports psychologist to their staff for the very first time.

The key to visualization is that your imagination must be vivid and detailed. To do this you must engage all the senses and duplicate the emotions you may feel: the background activity, the lights, the smells, the sounds you will hear, all of it. These mental images create a memory of that action. There are two theories that explain how it works:

1.) Psycho-neuromuscular Theory: vividly imagined events create the same neuromuscular responses as if you are having the actual experience.

2.) Symbolic Learning Theory: imagery can actually create a blueprint or a coding system of movement patterns in the central nervous system.

There is no greater example of the soundness of this theory than the story of Air Force Colonel George Robert Hall. Hall was shot down in Vietnam and was taken prisoner by the North Vietnamese. He was held at the infamous Hanoi Hilton, notorious for its mistreatment of American servicemen. He was held for seven years.

While locked up, Hall would visualize a full round of golf in his mind every day. His focus was so vivid that he could feel the warmth of the sun and hear the sound of birds singing. Colonel Hall would visualize the weather conditions, course conditions, clothes he was wearing, type of clubs he was swinging, balls, tees and even his playing partners. He imagined tying the laces on his golf shoes, taking two practice swings, deep breaths at address, and before each putt finding the proper line. Hall could visualize wind direction and green undulation. The Colonel would repair divots and ball marks as well as visualizing himself pulling the ball out of the hole, replacing the flag and carding his score. George Robert Hall visualized virtually every imaginable scene he could or would encounter on a golf course.

Remarkably, only one week after being released from seven years of confinement in a six square foot cell and without the benefit of physically practicing, Colonel George Robert Hall shot a career low round of 76 while competing in the Greater New Orleans Open.

So picture yourself succeeding at the action you're visualizing. Make sure that it is very positive and incredibly successful. The more vivid the better. See yourself performing efficient running, productive swings, sound catches and throws. And yes, allow yourself to imagine lining up after your championship game to receive your championship medal!

Visualize your goal! Back those thoughts with detailed and vivid imagery. Then when you are faced with reality it will feel familiar and you will be able to let your body go where your mind has already been!

35. EMOTIONS ARE POWERFUL

KEEP THEM IN CHECK!

"I don't want to be at the mercy of my emotions. I want to use them, to enjoy them, and to dominate them." Oscar Wilde

A pregame story for the biggest game of the year, an elimination game.

There can be no doubt that emotions play a large part in any sports competition. They create an energy that we feel in the pit of our stomachs as that big game approaches. They create the adrenalin that fuels us. Harnessing our emotions in the big game is the toughest challenge an athlete faces. Those who do are far more likely to succeed, those who give into them, more often than not will fall.

On Sunday night November 1, 2015, New York Mets pitcher Matt Harvey was the starting pitcher in game five of the World Series at Citi Field in New York. His team was down three games to one and facing elimination.

His job was to keep his team in the game. If possible pitch eight innings and hold the Kansas City Royals at bay so that manager Terry Collins could hand the ball to the Mets very successful closer Jeurys Familia. Harvey went out, harnessed his emotions and pitched the best game of his career; throwing only 18 combined pitches in the seventh and eighth innings and when he left the mound his Mets were ahead 2-0. The odds said New York had a 94% chance of winning the game.

As the Mets were batting Harvey was informed by his pitching coach that he was done and that Familia was going to close out the win and keep the Mets alive. It was here where Harvey's emotions took over. "No way" he said to his coach and he immediately went to his manager Terry Collins. "No way I'm coming out of this game" he said to his manager "no way." In the stands 45,000 Met fans were chanting "Harvey, Harvey, Harvey"!!! And it was here where Collin's emotions took over.

The Mets went out in their eighth inning and as Harvey emerged from the dugout, 45,000 Met fans went into a delirium. Harvey bounded to the mound and Royals centerfielder Lorenzo Cain stepped in. Harvey's emotions were now in control of him. His ball was still moving but his command of the ball was gone. Wild in the zone he walked Cain, who stole second on the first pitch. Eric Hosmer then doubled cutting the lead in half and he too would eventually score to tie the game. The Royals scored five runs in the top of the 12th inning to take the game 7-2 and the World Series four games to one!

Gentlemen, every athlete will feel that emotion, every athlete is faced with the challenge of dominating them, it is the champions who face them, embrace them, use them, harness them and dominate them. Tonight we take the field embracing our emotions, letting them fuel us, but we will stay within ourselves, we will harness them and we will dominate our emotions. AND WE WILL PREVAIL!!!!

https://www.youtube.com/watch?v=Pzxw_Q6tmog

https://www.youtube.com/watch?v=nR1YnJkZddc

36. LEARN FROM THE ANT

A LESSON IN TENACITY.

Tenacious- Not easily stopped or pulled apart. Firm or strong, extremely determined to do or accomplish something. A story on building mental toughness.

Ants never, ever quit! If they are going somewhere they will not be stopped. They will go over, under or through every obstacle. They will strive forever or they will die trying giving the ultimate sacrifice in never giving up. We can learn much from the ant.

A community of ants is called a colony, which is comprised of hundreds, thousands possibly millions of inhabitants. Each ant has its own special purpose with the vast majority responsible for protecting the queen. An ant has only 250,000 brain cells yet for their size they are among the most intelligent creatures on earth and they can lift up to 50 lbs. over their own body weight, making them among the earth's strongest creatures as well.

The average worker ant will live 90 days with their job being to build the colony and protect the queen; who will live from five to ten years. With this singularity of purpose they NEVER stop working; NEVER stop doing their job! They thrive in the summer but are always preparing for winter, their toughest months. Their focus and purpose is complete- to protect and defend the nest, to protect and defend the queen; and if they must, die for her. They never stop preparing for any negative event or possibility.

Gentlemen, mentally tough people master their shortcomings, master the negative events of a season or a game. Negatives and failure are part of the natural flow of the game, indeed of life; a natural way to success. Mentally tough people are never defeated by the games natural flow, they absorb them and, like the ant, they come back with a renewed sense of a singularity of purpose and rejuvenated tenacity! That type of effort and focus is what we need; stay focused, stay tenacious and we will prevail.

CHAPTER THREE

ADVERSITY—
IT HITS ALL PLAYERS AND ALL TEAMS

37. GENE KRANZ AND APOLLO XIII

FAILURE IS NOT AN OPTION

This is a great story of simply refusing to accept defeat. It is best suited to be used before a game when if you lose your season is over.

On April 11, 1970 at 13:13 military time, Apollo 11 launched from the Kennedy Space Center in Cape Canaveral, Florida. This was the third Apollo mission scheduled to put man on the moon. Jim Lovell was the commander of the flight, Jack Swigart, the command module pilot and Fred Haise would pilot the lunar module.

Gene Krantz, a former Korean War fighter pilot, was the flight director. The flight director is the man who sat in the big chair in Houston's Mission Control Center, overseeing dozens of staff who sat glued to their screens; each with a specific responsibility regarding the spacecraft, crew, and the mission. All data and information flowed through them into the headsets of Kranz who ultimately was responsible for all the final decisions.

They were 56 hours into the mission and 205,000 miles from earth when the unthinkable occurred. Responding to some "housekeeping chores" which were required before bedding down for the night, Jack Swigart flipped a switch to stir the oxygen tanks. A faulty switch caused an explosion that crippled the spacecraft.

Within an hour Kranz learned of the extensive damage to the ship. Not only was the mission to the moon lost but the hope of the crew returning home safely became "**near** impossible."

Flight director Kranz spoke to mission control calling upon them to "stay in the moment" and work the problem "step by step" for **"failure is not an option."**

What followed was the most remarkable spaceflight in the history of space exploration. Under Kranz's leadership, mission control encountered and conquered one problem at a time- Not enough power, not enough oxygen, life threatening CO_2 levels, no guidance system, loss of computer, three days of below freezing temperatures, severe damage to the mother spacecraft, possibility of a damaged heat shield and no parachutes.

After days of solving one life threatening problem after another, the moment of truth was at hand. When a spacecraft returns to the earth it goes through a communication blackout. This is caused literally by the fire the friction that returning through the earth's atmosphere creates. It is calculated almost to the second when communication can be expected to return. Apollo XIII entered their communication blackout that was expected to last three minutes.

The time for blackout was drawing near when command module pilot Jack Swigart said, "I know all of us here want to thank all you guys down there for the very fine job you did." Eighteen seconds later the communication blackout began. Everything possible that could be done was done and all that remained was the wait. Three minutes came and went, four minutes and still no word. A deafening silence hung in the air of Mission Control as the blackout approached five minutes and the worst possible scenario seemed to have occurred. After long grueling hours of doing everything possible to keep the spacecraft operable and the crew alive it appeared the crew was lost.

Suddenly the spacecraft appeared on the screen. Three red and white parachutes floating her softly to her splashdown just off the deck of the Iwo Jima. Apollo XIII was safely home!

Gentlemen, this is a must game for us! We will either continue our season or it will end on this baseball field tonight. We have been through a lot this year, we have endured injuries, defeats and the difficulties and challenges that a long season and the game of baseball will always bring. And WE HAVE ENDURED to this point. Failure is not an option tonight men. No matter what happens out there during this game we will persevere! We will grind out every pitch. We will overcome every obstacle. We will maintain our composure, we will stay focused and we will endure. We will prevail, we will pick each other up, we will win and we will bring each other home.

http://apollo13.spacelog.org/05:22:22:28/#log-line-512548

https://www.youtube.com/watch?v=WyZenck9WQg

https://www.youtube.com/watch?v=OZuUwcl_wT8

http://www.space.com/17250-apollo-13-facts.html

38. WE ONLY FAIL WHEN WE QUIT

ABRAHAM LINCOLN, OVERCOMING ADVERSITY

"The path was worn and slippery. My foot slipped from under me, knocking the other out of the way, but I recovered and said to myself, 'It's a slip not a fall'." Abraham Lincoln

This is a practice story about the "long haul" and developing an attitude that an individual will carry through life long after their playing days are over.

Perhaps the most iconic figure in all American history, Abraham Lincoln, endured a wide range of personal and professional adversity before assuming the arduous and near impossible task of leading a country split asunder by Civil War.

There may be no greater example of persistence and resilience than the 16th President, for through it all he refused to give up, or give in, He never saw quitting as an option and he simply endured.

Born into poverty, he became acquainted with adversity at an early age and it would revisit him throughout his life. He endured personal tragedy, professional failures and political losses and rejections at virtually every turn. He survived difficulties that would have swallowed lesser men but his determination, integrity, and character would simply not allow him to quit. Today he is widely recognized as the greatest President in the history of the United States of America.

1816- At the age of seven, his father lost a land dispute and was forced out of his home in Kentucky. His anti-slavery father moved his family to Indiana, a free state.

1818- His mother died.

1831- Working hard as manager of a store, he lost his job when the store's owner overextended himself and the store went out of business.

1832- Ran for the State Legislature and lost.

1833- Went into business with a partner and shortly after the business failed, his partner died. Lincoln assumed his partner's debt which he repaid in full.

1834- He was elected to the State Legislature.

1835- The love of his life, Anne Rutledge passed away.

1836- One month following Anne's death, he threw himself into his reelection campaign and won.

1837- Betrothed to Mary Owens, it comes to an end when she simply does not answer his letter.

1838- After reelection for the third time, he ran for Speaker of the House of the Illinois State Legislature and lost. In this same year he received his license to practice law from the Illinois State Supreme Court.

1839- He was elected a Presidential Elector for Illinois Whig Party and held the position for the Presidential elections of 1840, 44, 48, 52 and 56.

1842- He married Mary Todd.

1843- Lost in his bid to become the Whig candidate for Congress.

1846- He is elected to Congress as a Whig.

1849- He sought the job of Land Officer in his home state and was rejected.

1850- The Lincoln's second son, Eddie died at the age of four of consumption. (Tuberculosis)

1854- After receiving the most votes for the US Senate, but six votes shy of election, he withdrew from the race to insure that a pro-slavery democrat would not capture the seat.

1856- Unbeknownst to him, his name is placed in nomination for Vice-President of the new Republican Party. He does not win, receiving 110 of 363 votes.

1858- Although winning the popular vote as a member of the anti-slavery Republican Party, the democrats win majority in the Illinois State Legislature and name Stephen Douglas to the US Senate.

1860- He was elected President of the United States.

1862- His third son Willie dies of "fever" devastating Lincoln and his wife Mary.

1862- A few short months after Willie's death, he signs the Emancipation Proclamation elevating the Civil War to a higher plane as the freeing of the slaves now becomes an objective of the war.

1863- He delivers the Gettysburg Address considered by many the greatest speech in the history of the United States.

1864- He appoints Ulysses S Grant commanding general of all Union forces and stays with him through vicious criticism that he is "a butcher." Through it all Lincoln maintains simply, "he fights, he wins."

1864-1865- In late 1864 and into 1865 he leads, what many considered a lost cause as he works to pass the 13th amendment outlawing slavery. He succeeds!

1865- He is shot by an assassin five days after the surrender of Robert E Lee to Grant ending the war; and he dies the next day.

There may be no greater story of overcoming adversity and persevering to achieve unfathomable heights than that of Abraham Lincoln. We have had our ups and downs, we have had our failures... we have had our slips. But we cannot and will not fall! Not tonight men...Tonight we take our cue from the greatest president in history and we may slip but we will not fall, we get back up and take it!

39. REFUSE TO ACCEPT CAN'T

JOSHUA LAWRENCE CHAMBERLAIN

This story can be used in practice when working on the mental approach players need to develop or it can be used in a pregame situation when you face a team that is expected to beat you.

Born in Brewer, Maine in 1828, Joshua Lawrence Chamberlain was raised on the rocky terrain of Penobscot County Maine. The son of a Puritan minister he was ingrained with a work ethic and determination that carried him through his life.

Called Lawrence by his family, his education began at the age of 12 when he was plowing the family farm and encountered a bolder. The bolder was buried deep in the ground and after working for hours he went to see his father for help removing it. "Father" he said, "I've struck a bolder in the field and I CAN'T move it." His unsympathetic father simply replied "that field has to be plowed and that rock has to be moved." Young Chamberlain returned to the field, to his plow, and to continued frustration. Throughout the afternoon he tried to loosen the boulder and as the day was coming to an end he went back to his father. "Father, I have tried and tried to move the bolder and I simply CAN'T do it." Again his father showed no sympathy and emphatically instructed him. "Tomorrow you will move that rock!" "But how" replied the boy. "Move it, that's how!"

The following day, the boy was up early and before dawn was engaged with the daunting task of moving the immovable rock. He worked at it into dark and although he made some progress, at day's end the rock was still firmly in the ground. That night his father asked "How's the rock coming?" "Slow" replied the boy, "I just CAN'T get it loose," to which his father simply replied, "it must be moved." And that's all that was said. The next morning young Chamberlain rose before the sun and was back at the rock and its consternate challenge. By late morning he began to see some progress and as he did his confidence soared. His father watched from afar.

It was near dark when the rock was finally free and his oxen dragged it out of the hole. Elated he ran to his father shouting along the way, "Father, Father" and his father knew that his son had accomplished the seemingly impossible. Out of breath he exhorted to his father, "I did it, I did it!" Smiling, the elder Chamberlain took his son's face in his hands, "great work Lawrence" he said, "never, ever use the word CAN'T, because when you do you are already defeated, when that word comes into your head or off your tongue, you must know that your task is formidable and you must somehow, some way accomplish what you set out to do. Don't ever forget this." "I won't" said the smiling, weary boy, "I won't."

By the age of 20 Joshua Chamberlain was fluent in nine languages and teaching at Bowdoin College. When the Civil War broke out, he felt an overwhelming desire to serve his country but the college would not release him from his contract to do so. He applied for a leave of absence to study languages in Europe and when that was granted he promptly volunteered and was named Lieutenant Colonel, then Colonel of the 20th Maine Volunteers. It was in that capacity he found himself at a place called Little Round Top in Gettysburg, Pennsylvania on July 2, 1863.

Following a march of nearly 50 miles in two days, the 20th Maine was sent to a position at the end of the Union line. Chamberlain's instructions came through Colonel Strong Vincent of the 18th Pennsylvania, "Colonel, you are the end of the line and you must hold to the last...If you don't the whole line will cave and the Rebs will have us surrounded, understood?" "Understood" Chamberlain replied.

For nearly four hours throughout that brutally hot afternoon, the 20th Maine repelled one Confederate assault after another until they were literally out of ammunition. It was then that Captain Ellis Spear reported to the Colonel, "Sir we are out of rounds. We CAN'T hold them back if they come at as again." Chamberlain looked into the eyes of his captains who had gathered around him. "We're going to attack" he said to them and their collective faces became a mass of incredulity. "Sir?" said Spear. "They've got to be as tired as we are, they won't be expecting it," Chamberlain explained. And with that he ordered his men to fix bayonets, called for the bugle and led the charge down the hill. The Alabamians were on the run and when the battle ended; over 400 of them were taken prisoner, many being held by men carrying empty muskets. The hill was saved, the day was saved, indeed, the Union was saved!

Chamberlain received the Congressional Medal of Honor for his efforts at Gettysburg and he fought in 19 more battles. He received four citations for bravery, had six horses shot out from under him and was wounded six times. including a wound at Petersburg which nearly killed him and would plague him throughout his life. He was promoted to General and it was he who was chosen by General Grant to receive the surrendering Confederate Colors that ended the war.

A four time Governor of Maine and among other things, he became the President of his alma mater. He died in 1914 at the age of 85, of complications from a wound that nearly killed him a half century earlier; never having accepted CAN'T as an option.

Tonight we face a formidable, daunting opponent. Some of you have heard, we CAN'T hit that guy on the mound tonight. Some of you have heard we CAN'T match their speed on the bases or we CAN'T match their defense on the field or our pitcher CAN'T get them out! We've heard all week we CAN'T beat them. Tonight its one inning, one at bat, one pitch at a time. We keep focus, we execute and we will beat them.

LET'S GO MOVE AN IMMOVABLE ROCK! LET'S DEFEND AN UNDEFENDABLE HILL!

https://www.youtube.com/watch?v=ZL-5uyp44WA

40. TURNING A NEGATIVE TO A POSITIVE

JIM LOVELL—A FAILURE BROUGHT ME HOME

This story is about turning a negative into a positive and can be used as a practice team defining story or before a game.

Jim Lovell was an American astronaut. He was chosen in 1962 to be an astronaut for NASA's Gemini Program, which was the second step to the moon. In his career Lovell logged over 700 hours in space on four missions. His first Gemini flight was two weeks in orbit in what was predominantly an endurance test. He and fellow astronaut Frank Borman spent two weeks in orbit in a capsule that was not much bigger than a phone booth. This performance earned him command of Gemini's last flight.

The Apollo missions to the moon were next and Lovell commanded two of them. The first was Apollo VIII, which was the first time man had visited the moon. Although they did not land on the moon, they did get within 50 miles of the lunar surface. It was the Christmas season on earth and in with the world watching and listening, Commander Jim Lovell read from the book of Genesis while describing the incredible scene below him.

In April of 1970, with Jim Lovell in command, Apollo XIII blasted off on its way to become the third craft and crew to land on the surface of the moon. Two days in, a faulty oxygen switch caused an explosion that disabled the spacecraft. In what was nothing short of a miracle, Apollo XIII was returned safely to earth. *(See the story of Apollo XIII on page 89.)*

Jim Lovell was a man familiar with adversity. As a Navy aviator and test pilot his life consisted of facing adversity in life and death situations. In his early days as a flyer, he was lost over the Sea of Japan. In the darkness of night he could not locate his carrier. Unable to locate his carrier and running out of fuel, he came to terms with the fact that he would have to ditch his plane in the sea when the lights in his cockpit went dark. This confirmed to him his fate and a ditch landing in the Pacific Ocean was his only option.

As he was bringing his plane down he noticed a green fluorescent trail in the water. Many years later he explained that an aircraft carrier churns up algae as it plows through the ocean and it creates this fluorescent glow. Following that glow, he landed safely on the deck of his carrier. He never would have seen it if the lights in his cockpit had not shorted out. He said, "you never know what forces will come together to get you home."

Gentlemen, Jim Lovell lived a life as a pilot and astronaut that was defined by overcoming adversity. Adversity presents opportunities for amazing results and overcoming adversity, as a team and as individuals, is a huge part of this game. How we handle the adversity that comes our way will define us, as a team and will define you as men. Like Lovell we will embrace it, face it, overcome it, and it will bring us home.

http://www.space.com/20320-astronaut-jim-lovell-apollo-13-biography.html

https://www.youtube.com/watch?v=N91ogCGpYl0

41. BETWEEN A ROCK AND A HARD PLACE

ARON RALSTON-THE ULTIMATE GRINDER

This is a story of a special kind of courage, to be used before a game in which everything is on the line!

It was in late April when Aron Ralston was hiking in Blue John Canyon in Utah. He was by himself and nobody was aware that he had decided to take this particular hike. He was descending a slot canyon, which is a canyon that is about three feet wide and up to 100 or so feet deep, when a suspended boulder dislodged and crushed his hand against the canyon wall and pinned him there. Trapped in the canyon wilderness, he had two burritos and about 12 ounces of water.

He spent three days attempting to extricate his right arm from the 800 lb. boulder which held him. Dehydrated and delirious, on the fourth day he knew he would have to amputate his arm at the forearm to free himself. Using a two-inch pocketknife, he began experimenting with cutting through the flesh of his forearm and it was then he realized his knife would not be able to cut through his bones.

On the fifth day he was out of food and water. Now drinking his own urine, he prepared himself for death. He scratched on the sandstone walls his name, date of birth and presumed date of death. He videotaped his goodbyes to his family before drifting off to, what he believed would be, his final sleep.

When he woke the next morning, he was struck with an epiphany! It occurred to him that using torque from his trapped arm he could, in fact, break his arm, which would then permit him to sever off his arm. After breaking his arm, he completed the amputation in a little over an hour.

Not yet out of the woods, he climbed out of the slot canyon, rappelled a 65 foot sheer cliff and then began his hike across the canyon in the midday sun. He was eight miles from his truck. While hiking across the canyon he encountered a vacationing family and he was saved. Ralston lost 40 lbs. and 25% of his blood volume, but he was alive and he survived. He was saved six hours after amputating his arm.

Today he still climbs and one day hopes to reach the peak of Mt. Everest. A motivational speaker, he said many years later that if he had amputated his arm earlier, he would have bled to death and that he didn't see it as losing his arm, but taking back his life.

Gentlemen, there are situations which require a special kind of courage. Things occur in our lives which will force us to summon something within that we are not even sure exists. Tonight, as we take on this opponent, none of us is in danger of death: However, our season dies tonight if we do not prevail. No matter what transpires within the game, we will endure! Summon that special courage tonight men. Go deep inside and tap that place that will bring you to the apex of your performance. We do that tonight men, and we will prevail.

Ralston, Aron; *Between a Rock and a Hard Place* (Simon & Schuster)

Rollings, Grant (January 4, 2011). "'I smiled as I cut off my arm. I was grateful to be free'". *The Sun* (London).

http://www.nbcnews.com/id/5956900/#.VYmvNLtRHIU

42. PURPLE HEARTS, BRONZE STARS AND SUPER BOWL RINGS

ROCKY BLEIR

This is a story that can used in a practice in which you want your players to think about getting to the next level. To push themselves beyond the nagging little hurts and bruises any season brings. To reach inside and simply be better. It can also be used in a pregame situation as you may see fit.

A graduate of Notre Dame University in 1968, Rocky Bleir was a member the 1966 National Championship team and he was the captain of the 1967 squad. Not your prototypical running back, he was a 16th round draft pick of the Pittsburgh Steelers in the 1968 NFL draft.

He saw limited action in 1968, rushing the ball six times and catching three passes. And before the year would end he was drafted again, only this time by the US Army. He volunteered for service in Vietnam and in May of 1969 he shipped out with the 196th Light Infantry Brigade.

It was late August when he was on a recovery mission to retrieve the bodies of fallen comrades when they came under fire. Bleir was hit in the thigh by a North Vietnamese round which tore through the flesh but missed the bone. With a gauze wrapped around the wound, he made his way to his CO who also had been hit. While there, they came under fire again and a grenade was thrown which hit his CO in the back and rolled between Bleirs legs. The grenade exploded; shrapnel sprayed both the men, with Bleir taking it in his foot, leg and thigh. For his heroic efforts Rocky Bleir received the Purple Heart and the Bronze Star.

When he was finally evacuated, amidst rumors that both he and the captain had been killed, he was air-lifted to Tokyo where the first of many surgeries were performed on his foot and leg. The first procedure removed over 100 pieces of shrapnel, When all was said and done, he had lost part of his foot and was told that he would not have "the strength or flexibility to be a running back in the NFL." And that if he was lucky, "you might walk normally again."

Bleir NEVER accepted that prognosis. "When playing sports, on any level, even pickup games in the backyard, accidents happen, injuries occur," Bleir said. "Whether it's a broken arm, a twisted knee, a sprained ankle, we've all experienced it on one level or another, and then you kind of learn some lessons. And one of those is that, in time, these injuries heal and then you go back out and play again. So that was always my mindset. It wasn't like I had lost a leg," Bleir continued. "The damage impacted me, but my mindset was, 'Well, I've been there before.' I had a knee operation in college, had a lacerated kidney in college, bumps and bruises as a kid growing up, so to me it was just life, 'OK, I guess I've got to go through the rehab.'"

He was on injured reserve in 1970, and in 1971 he was placed on waivers. When he went unclaimed, he was on the Steelers taxi squad. Then to the utter amazement of head coach Chuck Knoll, Bleir made the team in 1972.

Playing special teams in 1972 and 73 he became a key part of the Pittsburgh offense and he would remain that throughout the decade-a decade which encompassed four Super Bowl Championships.

Bleir said, "If you're willing to reach beyond what you know you can do, then you can do almost anything."

We need you men to reach beyond what you know you can do. It's time for you to challenge yourself in ways you have not yet done. There is more in each and every one of you and it's you who has to go inside and get it. Push yourselves men, push yourselves to be better than you've ever been before! It's in you, you've got to just believe it! Remember, extraordinary outcomes seldom follow ordinary efforts. Make tonight's effort extraordinary.

https://www.youtube.com/watch?v=hJFtD1IYk3w

http://www.rockybleier.com/

http://www.foxsports.com/nfl/story/pittsburgh-steelers-rocky-bleier-recalls-vietnam-war-40-years-after-it-ended-043015

43. BATTLING BACK FROM THE BRINK

BEN HOGAN

This story is about battling back from the brink and overcoming bad breaks and individual circumstances. You define the brink. The brink of death, the brink of elimination, the brink of giving up. It can be used in a team context or an individual context and thus can be used in practice or before a game.

Long before there was Tiger Woods, there was a man named Ben Hogan. Hogan was known for a purity of striking the ball that is still talked about in golf circles today. He joined the PGA Tour in 1930 and went on to become one of golf's all-time greats. He retired in 1971 with 64 PGA wins which today ranks him fourth all time in wins. He is a four time US Open Champ, has garnered two green jackets, won the PGA Championship twice and he captured a British Open Championship as well. His total of nine major championships has him tied for fourth all-time.

However the measure of Ben Hogan goes far beyond his accomplishments on the golf course. The measure of Ben Hogan comes from the depth of his character and his ability to deal with the adversities and pitfalls that can befall one's life.

And it began for Hogan at the tender age of nine when he witnessed his father take his own life. This was years before the days of government assistants and not only did young Ben have to deal with the unspeakable horror of what he'd witnessed, but he now had to go to work to help his family survive. He did this by selling newspapers at a train station and then at 11, he became a caddy at a local golf course. It was here where his life was shaped. When he was not carrying bags, he was hitting golf balls and it has been said that he would do so often until his hands actually bled. His passion, determination and hard work paid off and he joined the tour in 1930.

It was the opening of the 1949 season and Hogan was on top of his game. He had 10 wins in 1948 including two majors and in early 1949 he already had two more wins under his belt and he had just been on the cover of Time Magazine. He was two weeks removed from his face gracing the cover of Time Magazine.

He and his wife Valerie, were headed down two lane Texas Highway 80 for the 500 mile trek home to Fort Worth. They hadn't gone but 10 miles when a Greyhound bus rammed into them head on. Hogan hurled himself on top of his wife before impact which saved them both as the steering wheel drove through the driver's side seat and Valerie was shielded by Hogan's body. Valerie managed to free herself and with the aid of a stopped motorist, they pulled Hogan out of the vehicle. It was 90 minutes before an ambulance arrived and when he finally reached the hospital, the extent of his injuries became known.

On the surface, his face was cut and bruised, and his left eye was practically swollen shut. He also had a fractured left collarbone, a double fracture of his pelvis, a broken ankle and a chipped rib. These turned out to be the least of his problems, as blood clots in his lungs nearly killed him; requiring abdominal surgery to tie off a vein. He was down to 117 pounds when he finally left the hospital on March 29th. His golf career in jeopardy.

Sixteen months later in June of 1950, Ben Hogan was back on the course competing in the US Open! Hitting a miraculous one iron shot on the 18th hole enabling him to par the hole and force a three way tie; Hogan emerged victorious in the 18 hole playoff the next day!

His remarkable re-birth found him win two majors in 1951 and then in 1953 he completed what was called his "Triple Crown" season winning, in order, the Masters, the US Open and the British Open. It marked the first time any golfer had won three majors in one year and that has only been duplicated once; by Tiger Woods in 2000!

Gentlemen, the game holds many adversities. Each of us will be victimized by this game, victimized by life in some way, some shape, some form. We cannot always control what happens to us. The ONLY thing we can control is how we respond to what happens to us! Ben Hogan had things happen to him of which he had no control. They could have eaten him up, destroyed him. But they didn't, because he controlled his response! He chose his path, he used them as a source of strength. Each adversity brings an opportunity for growth; the greater the adversity, the greater the growth opportunity Today we take the hard time we've been battling through and like Ben Hogan we grow into something better! Let's go do it!!!

https://www.youtube.com/watch?v=ExRTb9cmDLE

http://www.smithsonianmag.com/history/
hit-by-a-bus-how-ben-hogan-hit-back-24870580/?no-ist

44. MORE THAN A SURGERY, OF COURSE YOU CAN COME BACK!

TOMMY JOHN

This is a story that can be used in a practice and/or a pregame situation. It can also be used in a one on one situation with a player who is rehabbing from an injury.

Only Nolan Ryan and Cap Anson played longer in the big leagues than the 26 years that Tommy John played. Enduring adversities which would have swallowed most men, Tommy John is sports' epitome of adjectives such as guile, guts, heart, perseverance and moxie.

Recruited by the University of Kentucky to play basketball, the scouting report on the 18 year old southpaw was that he had a big league curveball in high school. However, with a fastball that hit 85-87 miles per hour, the prevailing thought was he "didn't throw hard enough."

In 1963 he made his big league debut at the age of 20 with Cleveland and following a 2-9 season he was traded to the White Sox. He spent seven years in Chicago with some good years and some not so good years and in December of 1971 it was on to the Dodgers where things were about to turn around.

John's lifetime mark before arriving in LA was 84-91 and he gave full credit to Dodgers pitching coach Red Adams for his turn around. "When I joined the club…I was still convinced that I had only a mediocre fastball and that I was going to have to depend chiefly on my breaking pitches to win ball games. But Red (Dodger pitching coach Red Adams) disagreed with me, emphatically." Adams told John that he had a good fastball, that while it was not going to set any speed records it had a lot of movement. "You'll get plenty of batters out with that." With a new found confidence, John began to get guys out with his "mediocre" fastball. The results were astounding. He turned into a top of the rotation pitcher, leading the National League in winning percentage two of the next three years.

Then on July 17, 1974 it all came crashing down in the midst of a 13-3 season. John's collateral ligament of his left elbow was completely ruptured and had to be replaced with ligament that was taken from his right wrist. This radical surgery was the first of its kind ever performed upon a pitcher and the odds were 100-1 that he would never return to the mound.

It would take two years before Tommy John returned to the mound on April 16, 1976. Following a 10-10 season, he became one of baseball's best pitchers reeling off seasons of 20-7, 17-10, 21-9 and 22-9. Making all the adjustments necessary under the guidance of teammate and kinesiologist Mike Marshall, John went on to win 164 games following the surgery that now bears his name!

Tommy John not only came back from his surgery, he came back better than he had ever been.

Gentlemen, this game is about battling back through adversity. It will test your desire, it will challenge your resolve and will bring you to your knees. The player who will endure is the player that is willing to commit and dedicate himself to whatever it will take to get you where you want to be. Tommy John took a risk and then fought a battle that he simply refused to lose. We define our own limitations gentlemen, challenge yourselves to do whatever it will take! Let today be the first day you take on that challenge in a way you never have before! Today we move toward the direction with our goal being better than we've ever been!

http://sabr.org/bioproj/person/cb280268

45. THE UNLIKELY BIG LEAGUER

JIM ABBOTT- SO WHAT IF I ONLY HAVE ONE HAND

Obstacle- A thing that blocks one's way or prevents or hinders progress.

"People will tell you that I overcame obstacles…maybe. But the truth is I was incredibly blessed in my life. More was given than was ever taken away."— Jim Abbott

This is a practice story about desire, dedication, will and how you perceive yourself and your situation!

Life by its very nature will be wrought with obstacles to overcome. They are as varied and as numbered as there are people in the world. When one takes on the choice to compete athletically they have also chosen to confront a myriad of "obstacles" that to many seem unique to the athlete. As the athlete confronts them they quickly learn how connected these are to the obstacles they will face in life. There is no man who ever competed at the major league level who overcame a larger physical obstacle than Jim Abbott. And the funny thing is, he did it because he never viewed his situation as an obstacle. His situation? He was born without a right hand.

Interested in sports at an early age Jim's folks tried to guide him to a sport where he didn't need to use his hands. The natural choice was soccer but Jim didn't like soccer and wanted to play what all the neighborhood kids played, baseball. And at a very young age he began to develop the remarkable eye hand coordination required to do with one hand what everybody else was doing with two. He spent thousands of hours throwing a ball against a wall and catching it and his dad helped him develop the glove switch which enabled him to throw and catch with the same hand.

At 11 years old he joined his first Little League team and in his very first game threw a no-hitter. From then on at every level he played he was told that his baseball career would end at that level. His high school coach doubted his ability to field the pitching position. Abbott not only pitched, he played first base and the outfield. His senior year he hit .427 and was 10-3 on the mound with a 0.76 ERA. Oh, and he was also the backup quarterback on the Flint Central High team; starting the last three games and throwing for 600 yards and six touchdowns and along the way was the teams punter averaging 37.5 yards a kick. He was drafted by the Toronto Blue Jays in the 36th round and he turned down their $50,000 offer to attend the University of Michigan.

His freshman year he went 5-2 and the following year he went 11-3 pitching the Wolverines to first place in the Big Ten and throwing a shutout in the NCAA Tournament. That same year he made the US National Team and threw a three hitter to beat Cuba in front of 50,000 fans. In the Pan Am games he won two games and did not give up an earned run. He topped off that year by garnering the Sullivan Award as the top amateur athlete in the country and the Golden Spikes Award as the College Baseball Player of the Year! The following year, his last in college, he became the first baseball player to be named Big Ten Athlete of the Year and he pitched a complete game win over Japan in the 1988 Olympic Games. That year ended with the Angels making him their first pick in the amateur draft (eighth overall) and he made the big league squad without any time in the minor leagues!

Jim Abbott's major league career lasted 10 seasons with four teams. In 1991 with the Angels, he finished third in the Cy Young Award voting, going 18-11 with a 2.89 ERA. He won 87 games in his career including 31 complete games and six shutouts! One of those was a no-hitter while pitching for the Yankees in 1993! Abbott's career was over at the young age of 31. When he retired, "experts" and "pundits" all speculated that the reasons for his loss of effectiveness were all tied to his "disability" catching up with him. For Abbott it was much simpler, his 95 mph fastball was now topping out at 90 and he was unable to make the adjustment from a "power" pitcher to a "finesse" pitcher.

Gentlemen, this game, indeed your life, will be filled with obstacles, filled with challenges, filled with difficulties to overcome. Some will be as a result of things you do, choices you make and some will simply find you. What you do with them is your challenge. How you perceive them is your challenge. How you handle them is your challenge.

What you do will be your decision and your choice but make those choices knowing that each adversity you face is an opportunity for growth. Growth as a player and growth as a person. The greater the adversity, the greater the growth opportunity. The greatest challenge exists where all challenges begin....in your mind. For it is there where all action begins!

https://www.youtube.com/watch?v=s-11R0f7I0g

CHAPTER FOUR

THE MIRACLE ON ICE: SO MANY STORIES WITHIN THE STORY

46. 1980 US HOCKEY TEAM

DO YOU BELIEVE IN MIRACLES?

Miracle- "An effect or extraordinary event in the physical world that surpasses all known human or natural powers and is ascribed to a supernatural cause."

This particular story is so powerful that it actually led to the creation of an entire chapter in this book. Originally slated to be used as a simple David and Goliath story, the magnitude of what unfolded in Lake Placid in 1980 dictated it was far more significant than something that simple.

It created this chapter of a team theme for a season and simply put, there is none better.

Your options with this story are many. If you choose the team seasonal theme, you may want to start your season by watching the movie with the team; you will then have a visual reference for the remainder of the season. You may find that the time will come when you may want to watch it again.

To gain the maximum impact upon your team, it is imperative that they understand the historical context in which this all took place. What was most striking to discover in our research is that, THERE TRULY IS NO COMPARABLE COMPARISION THAT CAN BE MADE TODAY. The reasons are explained within.

In the section marked Motivational Value Applying the Lessons various opportunities and situations are outlined. You may well find more. If you choose not to use the team seasonal theme; you certainly can pick and choose which of these nuggets you can apply to your team on an individual basis throughout the year.

The US Hockey team's gold medal performance in the 1980 Olympic Games in Lake Placid, New York provides an opportunity to motivate your team on several different levels. How and when you choose to use this story obviously depends upon your team and where you may find yourselves at any given point, in any given season.

There are a number of motivational stories which can be plucked from this story and used on an individual game, player, or team basis. However, it also provides an opportunity to set a theme for the entire season. Because it can be an all-encompassing team theme we chose to present here as it can be a powerful tool to set the tone from the first practice and then can be revisited throughout your season.

As a team theme the season should begin with the team watching the movie *Miracle*. This will provide a reference point for the entire season from which to springboard to all the stories you can touch upon throughout the year.

Their story opens the door to teach about: preparation, coming together as a team, believing in yourself and each other, accomplishing the seemingly impossible, rising to the occasion to seize the moment, mental toughness and focus, and working harder than one ever thought possible. It provides an opportunity to teach the value and significance of each contribution and it gives an unprecedented example of finishing the job and not letting a huge win on the way to a championship go for naught because of a job unfinished. It is a David and Goliath story like no other and it is a living example that the BEST TEAM is not necessarily comprised of simply the best players.

The argument can be made that this is the single greatest upset in the history of team sports competition. To understand it, explain it, and use it properly requires an understanding of it within its context in history.

In 1980, unlike today, the summer and winter games were played in the same year. The Cold War was in high gear between the USA and the Soviet Union and following the Soviet invasion of Afghanistan in 1979, President Jimmy Carter put forth the idea of boycotting the 1980 summer games in Moscow. For the first time in the history of the Olympics, politics threatened them.

What has to be emphasized and understood is the caliber of athlete who competed in those days were amateurs! There were no "Dream Teams", for any athlete who received any type of payment was banned from Olympic competition. Allowing professional players to play was against the rules. Therefore, the amateur pool in US hockey encompassed college players.

This rule gave a great advantage to athletes coming from what was known as the "Soviet Bloc." This consisted of communist countries who selected their players for the National Teams. These players were enormously talented and many of them had the ability to play in the National Hockey League. All they did was play hockey! They and their families were "taken care of" in every way possible. They were professionals in every sense of the word, but because they were the "National Team" they maintained their amateur status. This situation gave a decided edge to the Soviet Union and the Soviet Bloc for the better part of four decades.

THE SOVIET TEAM (RUSSIA)

The US team had defeated the Russians and won the gold medal in 1960 at Squaw Valley. A huge upset, this has been sometimes called the "Forgotten Miracle". The Soviets vowed that it would not be repeated and the entire country dedicated itself to that effort. They arrived at Lake Placid heavily favored to capture their fifth straight gold medal, dating back to 1964. From 1964-1976 their Olympic record was 27-1-1 and they had outscored their opponents 177-44. Four times they faced the US team, defeating them 5-1, 10-2, 7-2 and 6-2 respectively; for a collective 28-7 record. Simply put, Russia DOMINATED the US on the ice and had been doing so for 20 years.

Soviet domination was not merely confined to the United States team. The Soviets dominated virtually everybody and held their own against NHL teams and teams comprised of NHL superstars. In 1972 they played a "Summit Series" against a team of Canadian players who played in the NHL. It was an eight game series that took place in September with four games played in different Canadian venues and four played in Moscow. The Canadians won the series 4-3-1 while the Soviets outscored them 32-31 in the eight games. It was this series that established the caliber of the Soviet National Team in the eyes of the world. Although they enjoyed amateur status on paper, the Soviets played hockey 11 months out of the year. In 1974, a second Summit Series was held with players from the new World Hockey Association representing Canada. This time the Soviets prevailed winning four, losing one, and tying three.

In 1979, this series evolved into the Challenge Cup which was a three game series between the Soviets and an NHL team comprised not just of Canadian players, but NHL All-Stars. All the games were played at Madison Square Garden in New York and the Soviets prevailed two games to one, taking the decisive third game with a dominant 6-0 win.

Added to all of this is that minding the Soviet net was Vladislav Aleksandrovich Tretiak, who still remains one of the greatest goalies in the history of the sport! There was no doubt that the Soviet hockey team was as good as any hockey team in the entire world and many thought it was the best.

TEAM USA

The United States team begins with the coach, Herb Brooks. Brooks played for the University of Minnesota from 1955-1959. In 1960 he was a part of the "Forgotten Miracle" team which beat the Soviets for the gold medal. That is, he was a part of the team until the last cut. He was one of the 21 players to play and practice with that team until the very end. He was cut just one week before the games began and he watched them from his living room with his dad. When the US team prevailed he said to head Coach Jack Riley, "you made the right decision". In 1972, he returned to the Golden Gophers as their head coach beginning a stretch of excellence that included five trips to the Frozen Four and three National Championships in seven years.

The Gophers of Minnesota and the Terriers of Boston University had one of the fiercest rivalries in all of sports. It lasted for over 30 years and it reached its peak in the late 1970s. In the 1976 semi-final game, a bench clearing brawl erupted with 70 seconds remaining in the game. It took 30 minutes to restore order with Minnesota winning the game 4-2 and ultimately taking the National Championship. This game had serious ramifications as many players from both those teams tried out for and made the 1980 USA team. In fact, nine of Brook's Golden Gophers and four BU Terriers held 13 of the 20 roster spots.

It is hard to fully appreciate the task that awaited this hockey team. To gain some perspective, imagine a team of college football all-stars playing the reigning Super Bowl Champions. Think about it across the board, a college all-star baseball team, or basketball team taking on the reigning world champs in their respective sports. Now, after you wrap your mind around that consider this- the core of the Soviet Hockey team had been together for years. In the world of professional sports today, teams change from year to year and it is rare that a core of any given championship squad will remain together beyond three years. Therefore it is likely that there is no modern comparison which magnifies the depth and breadth of their accomplishment. In fact, a recent actuary study found that the likely Monte Carlo odds on the USA team winning that gold medal at 1000-1.

The first obstacle that Herb Brooks encountered was to convince the selection committee to accept his team. It was a 10 day selection process and there were many who did not agree with Brooks as he cut some very talented players, many with superior ability to those he kept. The next great task before him was to overcome the intense rivalry between the University of Minnesota and Boston University. This was played out in the persons of Rob McClanahan (Minnesota) and Jack O'Callaghan of Boston University who engaged in a vicious fight during an early practice. Brooks let them fight and used the opportunity to build his team. "If you are here to settle old rivalries, you're on the wrong team" he told them all. "We start becoming a team right now!" One of Brook's favorite expressions was "the name on the front of the jersey is a helluva lot more important than the one on the back." It was this early moment in this teams development that he began driving that point home. The actual birth of the team came they when they saw themselves as playing for the United States of America as opposed to their college. The first step towards Herb Brook's goal of gold.

Brooks had studied the Soviets for years and it was clear to him that one of the key factors to their success was their superior conditioning. He vowed to make sure his team would not fall because they were not in shape. Recognizing that "this team doesn't have enough talent to win on talent alone…No one has been willing to work hard enough to challenge the Soviets at their own game…We will work hard enough." He pushed them to their limits and beyond vowing each and every day that, "you may not be the most talented team in Lake Placid but you will be the best conditioned."

In the five months preparing for the Olympics, the American team played a total of 61 exhibition games. During these games

Brooks instilled in his players the wide open style of European play with daring, aggressive, physical contact. "You don't defend them…You take their game and shove it right back in their face." He knew that it was this style of play that would give them any type of chance against the Soviets. Their last exhibition game was played at Madison Square Garden in New York City. Their opponent-the Soviet national team, who handily trounced them 10-3. The pundits, the Soviets, the world, wrote them off.

THE OLYMPICS

In the first game, the USA played a favored Sweden team and although they looked impressive playing a very cohesive style of hockey, it looked like six months of grueling work and dedication would prove meaningless. Sweden led 2-1 with the seconds and US hopes ticking away. Goalie Jim Craig was pulled from the net and with 27 seconds to go, defenseman Bill Baker flipped a goal over the shoulder of Swede goalie, Pelle Lindbergh to give the US a 2-2 tie. The significance of this goal **CANNOT BE UNDERESTIMATED,** for without it, the Soviets would have won the gold medal on goal differential.

Things did not get any easier two nights later when they took on another Soviet Bloc team, the heavily favored Czechoslovakians. The Czechs were expected to win the silver medal behind the Soviets. The USA trounced them 7-3 and followed that up with wins of 5-1 (Norway), 7-2 (Romania) and 4-2 (West Germany). Winners of the pool, they advanced to the medal round where they would compete against Sweden, Finland, and the Soviet Union.

The Soviets skated their way to the medal round barely breaking a sweat, beating Japan (16-0), the Netherlands (17-4) and Poland (8-1) in the first three games. Things got a bit tougher the next two games but they prevailed against Finland (4-2) and Canada (6-4). The Finns and Canadians stayed with the Russians through the first two periods but superior Soviet conditioning prevailed in the end of both contests.

The stage was now set, the first round of the medal round would pit team USA against the Soviet Union on February 22, 1980; George Washington's 248th birthday.

THE GAME

Despite the fine performance of the American team in the first round of play, most still thought the outcome was a foregone conclusion. New York Times columnist Dave Anderson summed up the expectations of virtually everyone when on the day before this historic match he wrote; "Unless the ice melts, or unless the United States team or another team performs a miracle, as did the American squad in 1960, the Russians are expected to easily win the Olympic gold medal for the sixth time in the last seven tournaments."

For six months the US team had a clear and focused singularity of purpose. Every moment spent conditioning, every team meeting, every practice, every drill, every moment of their lives was spent preparing for this game.

Herb Brooks had been preparing for years. In fact, it could be said his preparation began in 1960. He was not a very talkative type of Coach. He was not one for lengthy pep talks. On this night he came into the locker room, looked into the eyes of his players and he uttered only 57 words.

"You were born to be hockey players. Every one of you. And you were meant to be here tonight. This is your time. Their time is done. It's over. I'm sick and tired of hearing about what a great hockey team the Soviets have. Screw 'em. This is your time. Now go out there and take it."

He turned and left the locker room.

A capacity crowd of 8,500 people jammed the *Field House* waving American flags and spontaneously breaking into God Bless America. They erupted in a resounding crescendo when the USA team appeared on the ice. Their moment had arrived.

The game opened, as many of them had, with the US team falling behind. The teams traded goals with the Soviets striking first at the nine minute mark. The US tied it five minutes later and with 2:26 left in the first period, Russia retook the lead. It was in that two minute and 26 second span that the possibility of a miracle manifested itself. As the closing seconds of that first period were ticking away, Mark Johnson sliced through two Soviet defenders and fired the rebound of Dave Christian's slap shot into the net to tie the game. There was one second left on the clock.

Immediately after the goal, Soviet coach Viktor Tikhonov replaced Tretiak in the net with backup goalie Vladimir Myshkin. This shocked everyone in the arena, especially the players on both sides. However, the Soviets were ignited and they peppered US goalie Jim Craig outshooting the US 12-2 in the second period. Only one of those shots got through however and the Russians carried a 3-2 lead into the third and final period.

At 6:47 of the third period, a high-sticking call gave the Americans a man advantage. In 27 minutes the Americans had mustered only two shots against the mighty Soviets. However, their aggressive play and the brilliance of goalie Jim Craig had kept those mighty Soviets at bay and the Americans still trailed by only a goal. That changed a minute and 52 seconds later when Mark Johnson fired a shot that went under Myshkin's glove tying the score. Ten minutes and 58 seconds remained in the game.

It was but a minute and 21 seconds later when team captain Mike Eruzione blasted a slap shot past a screened Myshkin giving the USA its first lead, 4-3. The American's were now 10 minutes from gold.

The Soviets responded with a ferocious flurry upon Craig and the Americans as Coach Brooks continued to implore his players to "play your game" and not fall into the trap of slipping into the defensive style which favored the experienced Russian squad. Superbly conditioned and filled with an unyielding confidence, the young Americans withstood the Soviet onslaught. With 33 seconds left, Craig kicked away a slap shot, another Russian slap-shot went wild leaving 20 seconds on the clock. And as Mark Johnson was digging in the corner ABC's broadcaster Al Michaels, began the most iconic 10 seconds in sports history. With the crowd in a frenetic delirium he began; "11 seconds, you've got 10 seconds, the countdown going on right now! Morrow, up to Silk. Five seconds left in the game. *"Do you believe in miracles?! YES!!!"*

The 8,500 patrons present rocked the *Field House* with the voice of 200,000,000 Americans as the stunned Soviets leaned on their sticks and watched in paralyzing disbelief. The impossible, the unimaginable, the unthinkable had occurred! And as the sounds of joy echoed from a little hamlet in New York and reverberated throughout the world, Herb Brooks made his way to "his boys" empty locker-room and wept with joy, the tears of champions!

THE GOLD MEDAL

The actual game to win the gold presented Brooks and his team with perhaps even a greater challenge than beating the Russians. It was two days after the defeat of the powerful Soviet team that they had to finish the job.

For months and in the case of Coach Brooks, years, the objective was to find a way to defeat the Soviets. All the energy, all the effort, all the focus was on beating the Russians. The energy expended in that effort and the successful result could not help but lead to the "we did it" mentality. The satisfaction, the gratification of accomplishing this most formidable goal left all spent and drained. However, the job was not finished.

The format that decided the medal winners was a round robin point system which, if the US lost, would keep them from winning any medal. If Finland won and Sweden beat the Russians, the USA would finish fourth and they would go home without a medal. And Finland was no pushover.

The gold medal game started as most of them did with the US trailing. It was 2-1 after the second period and Herb Brooks was sensing it all slipping away. If his boys did not prevail, this magnificent effort, this miraculous journey would become a footnote to history and the 1980 US Olympic Hockey team would be forever known as a team who simply did not get it done, despite a remarkable accomplishment.

Between periods in the locker-room Brooks gathered his men to impart the gravity of their situation and what was at stake. He looked at them said, "If you do not find a way to win this game in the last 20 minutes, you will take this loss to your bleeping graves…Your bleeping graves!"

Once again inspired by their coach, the Americans scored three, third period goals while holding the Finns at bay. The 4-2 win clinched the gold medal. During the ceremonies, the team captains stood on the podium while the American National Anthem played. In a spontaneous gesture, an iconic moment was born. With the anthem completed US captain Mike Eruzione called to his mates to join him on the podium and they rushed to do so. All 20 players gathered on that small podium and stood as one!

"Where we go one, we go all." Miracle complete!

MOTIVATIONAL VALUE; APPLYING THE LESSONS

As mentioned at this chapter's outset, this team, this story, provides an outstanding opportunity to motivate your team on so many levels and through a wide range of situations. It begins, as all teams do, with the team selection. When you are faced with the decision to cut the overtly talented malcontent who is selfish and does not value the concept of team. There is no better story in the history of sports that can illustrate the value of team and the lesson that a good, even great, team DOES NOT consist of simply the best or most talented players.

Hand in hand with that lesson is the lesson of coming to trust and believe in each other and how that elevates the belief in and confidence in the individual's ability as well. This mindset, this trust, creates a force within itself which strengthens the individual and emboldens the team. "Where one go, we go all."

The value of hard work, dedication, persistence and persever-ance was the hallmark of the 1980 US Olympic Hockey team. They provide a constant example of how simple work ethic can provide a singularity of purpose and can be called upon throughout the days, weeks and months of any given season, and even into and through the off season as well.

Woven within this remarkable tale of triumph is the concept of seizing the moment. "Great accomplishments come from great op-portunity." As any season in any sport progresses there will be the "Big Stage" moments. They do not have to necessarily be the cham-pionship moments that come for the few teams who advance that deep. They can be the rival game, the team record breaking game or any moment you choose to use as the "Big Stage" moment for your particular team in your particular season. Who will step up? Who will be the Jim Craig, the Mike Eruzione, or the Mark Johnson of your team? Who will be the one to answer your team's call of "Carpe Diem", and "Seize the Day?"

Each team, every season will present its own "Impossible Moment." That team which everyone believes is just simply impos-sible to defeat. The all-powerful perennial winner. The team that is always among the best. The team that your team has never beaten. The team that consistently competes for the league, district, confer-ence, state or even national championship. The "Miracle on Ice" al-lows any team the opportunity to have their time. Their 'not tonight" moment, the arrival of their time to "go out and take it"; despite the formidability of the opponent.

The tying goal against Sweden in the first game of the Olympics provides an opportunity to teach the lesson of the importance of ev-ery link in the chain of success. Without that goal none of it happens. Every event of every game within a season is linked to the success of every successful season of every successful team.

Following the victory over the Soviets the US team now had to face Finland to finish the job. With the format under which those games were played Finland could not only keep gold from the Americans but could literally keep them from any medal at all. The mental toughness, focus and effort the American team needed to muster to finish the job may be unprecedented. With the months of focus and effort targeting the Soviets, the "we did it" factor had to be overcome in only 48 hours.

The Miracle on Ice is the greatest upset in the history of sports and it is likely that the confluence of forces which brought it about will never happen again. However it lives as a story which can motivate athletes around the world and teach them the lessons of competition and the ingredients required to bring about miracles!

https://www.youtube.com/watch?v=qSkc6c35A4Q

http://www.nhl.com/ice/news.htm?id=704235

http://truesportsmovies.com/other-sports/miracle/

http://www.nydailynews.com/sports/hockey/u-s-ties-27-baker-goal-buoys-medal-chances-2-2-article-1.2023427

http://rangers.nhl.com/club/news.htm?id=518774

CHAPTER FIVE

THE BIG GAME

47. THE RUMBLE IN THE JUNGLE

ALI-FORMAN- TAKE SOME HITS THEN POUNCE.

This is a story to use before a game which you know you are overmatched by the opponent's talent and it will require the absolute best from every member of your team. There is no room for error as you are the decided underdog.

They called it "The Rumble in the Jungle" and it took place in Kinshasa, Zaire on October 30th, 1974. It was the fight which put Don King on the map as a promoter, promising each fighter the ungodly sum of five million dollars. And it was the fight that established, once and for all, Muhammad Ali as 'The Greatest."

Forman was the reigning World Heavyweight Champion having knocked down Joe Frazier six times in two rounds to take the title in a second round TKO in January of 1973. He had also stopped Ken Norton in a second round TKO in March of '74'. It was these two fighters who were responsible for robbing Ali's invincibility, both having defeated him.

The 25 year old was not merely the Heavyweight Champ, he was a force boxing had never seen. He was 40-0 and thirty of those fights had not gone past three rounds!

Muhammad Ali, on the other hand, was three months short of his 33rd birthday and many believed he was at the end of his career. All of this was not lost on the Las Vegas bookmakers who installed Foreman, the young champion, as an 8-1 favorite.

Scheduling the fight in Africa brought a worldwide attention that boxing had never experienced. Ali was as brash as ever, animated, glib and confident. He openly talked of how he would defeat Forman and become only the second heavyweight in history to regain his title.

His camp was not so sure. In fact, there were some among them that thought Ali would not only lose, but be destroyed; and some even feared for his life.

Ali had a plan and in the second round he put it in play. Knowing that his young foe had not gone deep into many of his fights, his plan was to let him punch himself out. He did this in a most unconventional way-going against the ropes. It went against every boxing strategy, a fighter should never let a solid puncher corner him on the ropes. And it took away from Ali his strength, his feet and his ability to move-to "dance."

With his corner consistently screaming to him to "Get off the ropes", Ali leaned on them absorbing Forman's mighty blows and when Ali counterpunched, many were with his right hand also counter to standard boxing strategy, as virtually all right hand punchers lead with their left hand.

As the fight progressed through the third, the fourth, the fifth and sixth rounds and Ali continued to lean on the ropes, Forman, now arm weary, was showing signs of fatigue. In the seventh round, Forman mounted one last concerted effort to knockout boxing's aging legend. In Forman's words, "I hit him hard to the jaw and he held me and whispered in my ear, is that all you got George? I realized, this ain't what I thought it was." [1]

In round eight Ali made his move and blasted Forman with a barrage of punches, the last a left hook that sent the invincible young champ to the canvas. He wobbled to his feet at the count of nine, but with two seconds remaining in the round the referee counted him out and Muhammad Ali had once again, done the impossible.

Following the fight, Ali coined his strategy the "Rope a Dope." Writer Norman Mailer, once a boxer himself, lent this more scientific explanation in his book *The Fight*, which far more illustrates the genius of Ali. "Standing on one's feet, it is painful to absorb a heavy body punch even when blocked with one's arm. The torso, the legs and the spine take the shock. Leaning on the ropes, however, Ali can pass it along; the rope will receive the strain."

Muhammad Ali was clearly physically overmatched in this fight! He was nearly a decade older and could not match the physical strength of his opponent. Undaunted, he found a way to hang around, and when he saw his opportunity he took it. He hung around long enough to wear out his foe and then pounced when he knew he could take him.

Tonight we may be physically overmatched, we may not be as big or as strong as them, we may not be as fast, but we know how to play! We know we're in for a long fight so let's go out and "Rope a Dope"! Hang in and battle, battle, battle; keep the damage to a minimum and then pour it on and beat them!

Shortlist.com

https://www.youtube.com/watch?v=bVseoF1-p3M

48. HOW DO YOU EAT AN ELEPHANT? ONE BITE AT A TIME

TAKING ON THE BIGGER OPPONENT.

This is a pregame story to be used against a formidable opponent. The opponent that may seem impossible to beat; that won't roll over and go away; that will absorb hits, effort and keep on coming at you. The opponent that requires peak performance from start to finish regardless of the score. It will work to keep your team focused in the moment: one pitch at a time, play by play, point by point!

Often when players look at the big picture they feel overmatched and can lose the game before it even starts. This will help them get their focus and see the game one pitch at a time, one at bat at a time, one out at a time, one inning at a time.

Gentlemen, there is a tale that comes from the Serengeti Plains of Tanzania, Africa. And it comes from the days when elephants were a source of food. There once was a man who was the smallest man in the village. He was often the source of ridicule and scorn, for he was only five feet six inches tall and weighed 110 lbs. One particular day when he was being taunted about his diminutive stature he chided back that he was "equal to them and could do anything that they could do and even better."

The village eating contest was coming up and the chiders challenged him to enter. This seemed absurd, for the contestants in the yearly contest were the biggest and strongest men of the village; this year's challenge was to consume an entire elephant in one sitting. The man had had enough and he accepted the challenge.

The day arrived and the entire village gathered as was the custom. The man was laughed at and ridiculed as he took his place among his very large challengers. The contest began and all of the men began cutting pieces off the roasted elephant. The man began slicing and dicing the pachyderm and he did not stop. Three hours later, to the amazement and astonishment of all, the little man finished, while the others still had large parts of the elephant in front of them.

When he was asked how he did it, he said, "While my opponents were ferociously attacking the massive beast; tearing off large chunks of meat and gobbling them down, I simply diced it up in controllable portions and methodically ate him, one bite at a time."

Now you direct your attention to the other team.

"Men, there's an elephant over there. They may be bigger and faster than we are but you know what? That doesn't matter because tonight we eat that elephant one bite at a time. One pitch at a time, one at bat at a time, one out at a time, one inning at a time. And three hours from now, that elephant will be gone!" You hungry men? I know I am, let's go get that elephant, one bite at a time."

You will be surprised how the team will respond to the silliness of the concept of eating the elephant!

It is very important that a coach prime the pump when a good thing happens and can start with the first out of the first inning; acknowledged with a comment, "We just ate the tail." With the coaches priming the team will pick up the concept as pieces of the elephant "disappear" throughout the game.

49. FINDING A WAY TO WIN (MERKLE'S BONER)

JOHNNY EVERS

This can either be a pregame or practice story but may be most effective in practice. It is a story of how a player can help win a game by simply paying attention to what is transpiring on the field. Seeing the game in its entirety. A player does not even have to be playing to help the team win. He could pick up a sign, notice a pitcher tipping his pitches, picking up pitch calling tendencies and assist the team in a host of other ways. Every player on each roster can have an impactful role if they want it.

On September 23, 1908, the NY Giants were playing the Chicago Cubs at the Polo Grounds in New York. The Cubs and Giants were among the best teams in baseball. With two weeks left in the season these teams were tied for first place. It was the bottom of the ninth inning of a 1-1 tie and there were two outs. Giant's leftfielder Moose McCormick was on third base and Fred Merkle, the Giants 19 year old rookie first baseman, was on first. Shortstop Al Bridwell singled to center field scoring McCormick with the winning run and, as was the custom back in the day, the fans swarmed the field.

Not so fast.

Cubs Hall of Fame second baseman Johnny Evers kept his eye on Merkle running from first. "He jogged halfway to second, "I saw him stop, glance at the fans pouring out of the seats and start for the clubhouse beyond right field." Realizing he still had a play at second, Evers yelled to umpire, Hank O'Day that Merkle didn't touch second and then called for the ball from centerfielder, Solly Hofman. Giant's pitcher Joe McGinnity, who was coaching first base that day, saw what was happening, intercepted Hofman's flip to Evers and heaved it away into the crowd. Undaunted, Evers went after the ball and after struggling with several Giant fans, retrieved it, ran and stepped on second base, theoretically forcing Merkle and negating McCormick's run which won the game; thus leaving the score tied at one. Unable to clear the field, Umpire O'Day called the game due to darkness, leaving the game tied.

Great controversy ensued with the final decision being made over a week later on October 2nd in which the league upheld O'Day's decision. And when the Giants beat the Braves on the last day of the regular season, the game had to be replayed on October 8th to decide the National League Champion. The Cubs prevailed 4-2 and went on to their third World Series in a row! They won that too and have not won it since.

The keen eye of Johnny Evers made that possible. Johnny Evers' coolness in the midst of chaos, made that possible. The determination of Johnny Evers made that possible. Tonight's game will require that kind of attention to detail; that kind of coolness amidst chaos, that kind of determination! Which one of you is going to be Johnny Evers when their Fred Merkle falls down?

50. CARPE DIEM —
RISE TO THE MOMENT

REGGIE JACKSON

This is a story to use before a big game on the big stage.

They called him "Mr. October" because he loved the stage, and the bigger the stage, the more he loved it. In baseball the stage is no bigger than Yankee Stadium in New York in the post season. However in October of 1977, the stage had not been kind to Reggie Jackson. In fact, on October 9th, the Yankees found themselves in a winner take all game five of the ALCS in Royal Stadium in Kansas City. And with Royals lefty Paul Splittorff on the mound, Reggie found himself on the bench for the biggest game of the year. Having produced but one hit in 14 ALCS at bats, manager Billy Martin inserted right handed swinging Cliff Johnson in the DH spot. Reggie watched as the Royals took a 3-1 lead into the eighth inning. Six outs from elimination, Willie Randolph singled and Splittorff was replaced by right-hander Doug Bird and following a strike out by Thurman Munson and a single by Lou Piniella; Martin called upon Jackson with men on first and third. An RBI single made it 3-2 and ignited the Yankees comeback which ended in a 5-3 win and New York's second consecutive trip to the World Series.

Jackson loved the pressure and in fact he thrived on it. Calling himself, "the straw that stirs the drink" when it all was on the line he wanted to be the man on the spot and in the spotlight! He earned his nickname by being one of the most clutch performers in the history of October baseball!

However, nothing could prepare the baseball world for what would take place just nine days later!

It was game six of the World Series and the stage was Yankee

Stadium as the Dodgers had forced a return to New York with a 10-4 win at Dodger Stadium in game five. Jackson had homered in his last at bat in game five; a seemingly meaningless shot as it simply made the final score 10-4. However in reality, it was a prelude to history.

The Dodgers took a 2-0 lead in the first inning and Reggie led off the second inning with a walk, He scored moments later when Chris Chambliss tied things up with a homer. LA retook the lead 3-2 in the third on a Reggie Smith home run and it remained that way until Jackson came to the plate in the fourth following a leadoff single by Thurman Munson. Jackson deposited Burt Hooten's first pitch into the upper deck in right field and the Yankees led 4-3. The Yankees would never trail again but Reggie Jackson, Mr. October, was far from finished. He came to the plate again in the fifth. It was 5-3 and Willie Randolph was on first. It was Elias Sosa on the mound this time and he threw his first pitch, and this time Jackson hit a laser on a line that reached the right field grandstand in about one half a second and the Yankees now led 7-3.

The Yankee fans were in a frenzy as Yankee Stadium was now in a carnival atmosphere for their beloved Bronx Bombers stood on the precipice of a return to glory! It had been 15 years since they had won a World Series, their longest stretch without a World Series win since their first one in 1923.

When Reggie Jackson stepped in to lead off the eighth inning, the frenzy hit a fever pitch. The Yankee Stadium scoreboard continually flashed REGGIE! REGGIE! REGGIE! And the fans chanted his name! Smiling Jackson stood in and awaited Charlie Hough's delivery. It was his patented knuckleball and Reggie swung and as soon as it left the bat a gasp went up in the crowd as his majestic shot traveled deep into the centerfield section 450 feet away.

That blast completed the remarkable feat of four home runs on four pitches in two games. It tied Babe Ruth as the only man to hit three home runs in a World Series and it broke the Babe's record of four home runs in a single World Series, it was his fifth. And it sealed the World Series win for the Yankees. Mr. October was the Series MVP.

Tonight, we take our biggest stage, which one of you wants to be the straw that stirs the drink? Who wants to be the one on the spot when it's all on the line? Which one of you will thrive on the pressure? Whose moment of greatness awaits?

Tonight, let's play like CHAMPIONS!

https://www.youtube.com/watch?v=hDMYVtzHGuI

51. ALWAYS BE READY

FRANCISCO CABRERA

This is a story for your role players, the players on the bench who may or may not be called upon during the game.

His name is Francisco Paulino Cabrera and he would play only 196 games in his entire five year major league career. He made but 374 plate appearances, garnering a mere 89 hits, and hit .254 with 17 home runs and 62 RBI.

He was a backup catcher, a backup first baseman and Baseball Reference lists his primary "position" as pinch hitter. But his moment, ah yes HIS MOMENT came just eight minutes before midnight on October 14, 1992 in Atlanta-Fulton County Stadium before 51, 975 fans and millions more on TV!

Coming out of spring training in April of 1992, Cabrera made the Braves squad, and was called upon to pinch hit four times in April with one of them resulting in a game tying homer against the Reds. However within two weeks he found himself bound for Richmond Virginia and the Braves AAA affiliate in the International League where he would spend his summer.

By the time he returned on September 13th the Braves were coasting in the NL East; playing out the string waiting to see if it would be the Pirates or the Expos who would challenge them for the right to play in the World Series. Cabrera was called upon to pinch hit eight times the last two weeks of the season and when the season came to an end his totals read, 11 plate appearances, 10 at bats, 2 runs scored, 3 hits, 2 home runs, 3 RBI, 1 walk, 1 strikeout for a batting average of .300. Nothing in his line of performance gave the slightest hint or indicated the impact Francisco Cabrera was about to make on the Atlanta Braves franchise.

The Pirates prevailed in the NL East and Atlanta was installed as heavy favorites to defeat them and go on to the World Series. The pundits appeared correct when the Braves won game four 6-4 to take a commanding three to one advantage in the series. However the Pirates prevailed in game five in Pittsburgh and in at Atlanta two nights later scored eight runs in the second on their way to a 13-4 rout setting up the winner take all game seven.

Pittsburg led 2-0 when Braves third baseman Terry Pendleton led off the ninth with a double down the right field line bringing up Dave Justice who hit a ground ball to second base; which Gold Glove winner Jose Lind booted putting men on first and third. Sid Bream walked and for the second time in the game the Braves had the bases loaded with nobody out. Stan Belinda replaced Drabek and the first Braves run was plated when Ron Gant lined out to left field. The bases were reloaded when Damon Berryhill walked bringing up pinch-hitter Brian Hunter who popped out to second.

Down to their last out, with the winning run on second base, Braves skipper Bobby Cox called upon Francisco Cabrera. He of only 10 big league at bats all season, he who had but one at bat in the entire series now held the entire Braves season in his hands. Cabrera lined a Stan Belinda pitch into left field for a single scoring Dave Justice easily to tie the game; and when gimp kneed Sid Bram chugged around third and slid safely home ahead of Barry Bonds' throw, the Atlanta Braves were the National League Champions.

Francisco Cabrera broke the collective hearts of the city of Pittsburgh while becoming an Atlanta Braves icon. In a franchise that claims the likes of Henry Aaron, Eddie Mathews and Warren Spahn, the journeyman utility guy who made but 374 plate appearances in his entire career is as revered as any of them simply because his moment came and he captured it!

The utility player, the pinch hitter has the toughest job in all of baseball. Called upon to prepare and be ready for something that may not happen and as often as not, does not happen. Standing at the ready requires a mental toughness like no other. Which one of you tonight will be ready, which one of you tonight will capture your moment, as Francisco Cabrera captured his?

https://www.youtube.com/watch?v=c3WtSKEMUio

https://www.youtube.com/watch?v=FgjIVvEQo_o

52. SEIZE THE OPPORTUNITY, IT MAY NEVER COME AGAIN

DAN MARINO

This is a story to use when your team gets into the playoffs. When to use it and at what stage of those playoffs you choose to use it depends upon the history of your individual program.

Dan Marino quarterbacked the Miami Dolphins for 17 seasons. Nine times he went to the Pro Bowl, three times as a first team selection. His name is sprinkled throughout the all-time quarterback leaders in virtually every category in both the regular season and the playoffs. In 2005 he was inducted into the Pro Football Hall of Fame in Canton Ohio!

In his second season in 1984, Marino rewrote the record book throwing for 48 touchdown passes and over 5000 yards! He led Miami to a 14-2 record and then through the destruction of Seattle in the first round of the playoffs 31-10 setting up the AFC Championship Game in his hometown of Pittsburgh.

The young brash quarterback outdid himself, throwing four touchdown passes and beating the mighty Steelers 45-28 with an astounding quarterback game rating of 135.4. Next came the San Francisco 49ers in Super Bowl XIX!

Arriving in San Francisco for the Super Bowl, Marino announced "The Terminator is here", a pun from the popular Arnold Schwarzenegger movie of the same name. However the Super Bowl was not to be. Although the Dolphins led 10-7 after the first quarter, the remainder of the game belonged to Joe Montana and the 49ers. Montana led them to a 38-16 victory!

The vast majority of NFL pundits believed that Super Bowl XIX was but the first of what would be many Super Bowl appearances for Marino and his Dolphins. One of Marino's favorite targets, wide receiver Mark Duper said "I'll never forget when we arrived there at the Super Bowl. I was like, we better get used to this. We'll be here the next three, four, five years." However it was never to be! Dan Marino and his Dolphins NEVER returned to the Super Bowl. In fact the Dolphins have not been to the Super Bowl since that day.

Reflecting on it 30 years later, Marino remembered "the disappointment.....I wanted to play that game again the next day....fix the mistakes." "I always thought I'd be back....Several times.....I was young." His advice to young athletes, "Take advantage of your opportunities....Take nothing for granted!"

We are fortunate to be here tonight! We've worked hard and we deserve it! Look around here men, recognize how special this is and how difficult it was to get here. Seize this opportunity now to become the champions which we strive to be! Go get it and above all....Enjoy every moment!!!!

https://www.youtube.com/watch?v=yLO0q8e5_LI

53. REVEL IN THE MOMENT, TAKE NOTHING FOR GRANTED

KEN BRETT- TAKING OPPORTUNITIES

This is a story that you can use in two different ways. From a team perspective, it is a lesson in appreciating where you are at. In that vein it can best be used when your team has reached "post season."

It can also be used in a one-on-one situation when you have an extremely talented player to whom the game appears to come easy. Brett's story of unfulfilled potential is poignant.

His name was Ken Brett and today he is best known for being the older brother of Hall of Famer George Brett. However, George himself would tell you that Kemmer, as his family called him, was better than he.

A left-handed pitcher and centerfielder in high school he went 33-3 and hit .484 throughout his prep years. Labeled with, what he would later call "the curse of unlimited potential"; he was the Red Sox first pick (fourth overall) in the second ever amateur draft of 1966. A $100,000 Bonus Baby, (huge money for the times) 1967 found him pitching in the Carolina League and the Eastern League, where he pitched a combined 189 innings going 14-11 with a 2.00 ERA and 225 strikeouts.

In September of that year he was called up to the Red Sox, who were in the midst of what today remains the closest pennant race in history. He made his big league debut nine days after turning 19. The kid caught the eye of Carl Yastrzemski who called him "the next Sam McDowell" (three time 300+ strikeouts in a season) and catcher Elston Howard said he "threw as hard as Sandy Koufax."

The Red Sox prevailed in that pennant race and Ken Brett became the youngest pitcher to pitch in the World Series, a distinction which he still holds. He appeared in two contests faced five batters gave up no runs, no hits, walked one and had one strike out.

Ken Brett pitched for 14 years in the Big Leagues never fulfilling his "unlimited potential." He did pitch on 10 different teams and was an All-Star with the Pirates in 1974 and he pitched in the NLCS in both '74 and '75'; he never made it back to the World Series. When his playing days were over he once commented, "I only wish I was old enough to appreciate what I was involved with at such a young age."

Men, we are embarking on our playoff run. We have worked hard and succeeded in making it this far. Take nothing for granted fellas, we have accomplished a lot but there are no guarantees in this game. We will play each game, one pitch at a time, reveling in every moment we are here and taking the opportunity to give each second we have our very best effort! Enjoy it gentlemen and use this opportunity to shine!!!!!

"THE CURSE OF UNLIMITED POTENTIAL"

The following can be used in a one-on-one situation with the player who is not "living up" to his potential.

Ken Brett had a 14 year major league career. He was by all standards a mediocre pitcher. He was 83-85 with a 3.93 lifetime ERA. He had an all-star season and believe it or not, he was so good as both an outfielder and a hitter that some folks talked about the Yankees drafting him to replace Mickey Mantle who was nearing the end of his career.

Why did this athlete not become a super star? There is more than one reason for sure but it might simply be that he was so good, always so much better than most that he never developed the wherewithal to cope with the failures of the game. Maybe he never figured out that he needed to work hard.

It really does not matter why, what matters is that he never fulfilled his enormous potential.

You have enormous potential, and you need to learn and come to terms with the fact that this game will bring you to your knees, no matter how good you are! You must develop the mental toughness to battle throughout that and you have to know that the next best player is always right around the corner and he wants your spot. NEVER be outworked!

http://sabr.org/bioproj/person/5e904106

http://www.amazon.com/1967-Red-Sox-Impossible-Baseball/dp/1467120936/ref=sr_1_1?ie=UTF8&qid=1435071755&sr=8-1&keywords=1967+red+sox&pebp=1435071762514&perid=170T8NEWQJODBEM62WTW

54. SQUEEZE-NEVER LET UP

THE PYTHON NEVER LETS UP

A story for the team when a complete total focused effort is required for a formidable opponent.

The rattlesnake may well be the most well-known poisonous reptile on the planet. Made famous as costars in scores of Western movies, they are dramatic. They rattle their tails as they coil, raise their necks and then they strike, at times from distances as long as their body. A nine footer can successfully hit a prey that is nine feet away. They are swift, they are accurate and they are deadly. However, the reality is that there are approximately 8000 venomous snake bites in a year and since 1990, only 12 have resulted in death.

The Python on the other hand is far more efficient at netting its prey. He is stealthy, he is clever, he is deliberate and he is deadly. Wrapping his body around its prey it simply waits, buying his time and letting his foes fear, his foes energy work in his favor. He waits for his foe to take a breath and with each breath he squeezes, a little harder, until the breath is literally squeezed out of him. Slowly, deliberately and with a focus and patience that comes from knowing he will succeed. With each squeeze, he is closer to victory as his opponent struggles for air until he succumbs.

Tonight gentlemen, we must be that python. We need a complete and total focused effort. We must not simply apply a quick hit and then think those guys over there are going to roll over and die. No sir! We must be like that python, we must wrap ourselves around them and pitch by pitch we squeeze a little harder and slowly, deliberately we will squeeze until victory is ours!

http://www.aafp.org/afp/2002/0401/p1367.html

55. EMBRACE AND KNOW YOUR ROLE...BE READY

DAVE ROBERTS

This is a great story to use with your bench players. It can be prefaced with how important it is that they stay focused upon what is going on at all times; for when their moment comes it could well be when the game, indeed the season may be on the line. It can be used in practice or pregame and may be most effective as a practice story which you can reference throughout the season.

It was the fourth game of the 2004 ALCS. The Yankees held a three games to none lead in the series and were ahead 4-3 in game four. It was the ninth inning and Mariano Rivera was on the mound. The greatest closer in the history of baseball needed to get three outs and the Yankees would vanquish the Red Sox in four games and head back to the World Series for the second year in a row.

Red Sox first baseman Kevin Millar, led off the ninth and worked a walk, and as he was making his way to first base, manager Terry Francona looked to Dave Roberts and simply winked at him. When Millar reached first base, Roberts bounded out of the dugout as Fenway Park announcer Carl Beane informed the crowd that Dave Roberts was running for Kevin Millar.

Roberts took first base and the chess match began. Roberts getting his lead, Rivera looking over, holding the ball; the first throw, Roberts dove back safely. A bigger lead, another throw over, Roberts again dove back but this time he was nearly thrown out. Another lead, Rivera holds, and holds, and holds and then the pitch. Roberts is off with a great jump and he slides headlong into second beating Jorge Posada's throw by a whisker. Sox third baseman Bill Mueller, followed with a single that scored Roberts and tied the game.

The rest, as they say, is history. David Ortiz blasted a two run homer in the 14th inning to keep the Red Sox alive. The following night it was Ortiz again only this time with a game winning single in the 14th and it was back to New York where the Red Sox took games six and seven becoming the first (and to date only) team to be down three games to zero in a League Championship Series and come back to win it! And it all began with Dave Roberts.

Dave Roberts played in 832 major league games in 10 seasons. Forty five of those came in 2004 with the Boston Red Sox who acquired him from the Dodgers on July 31st. He stole a whopping total of five bases for them that season. Yet, when his manager called upon him when the season was on the line, he was focused, he was ready and he executed! In 2006, Dave Robert's steal was recognized in the Red Sox Hall of Fame as one of the franchises most Memorable Moments and it is said today Dave Roberts cannot buy a dinner in Boston.

Gentlemen, baseball is a chain of events and you never know what the key event may be. So tonight, you players who are not in the game, know your role, stay focused, stay ready and when your moment comes execute, for it may well turn into our most important moment of the season!

https://www.youtube.com/watch?v=VQ-VM4UDq-E

CHAPTER SIX

WORK, PREPARATION, ADJUSTMENTS

56. GOING THE EXTRA MILE AND BEYOND

BILL SHARMAN—PERFECT PRACTICE LEADS TO SUCCESS.

*"Hard work doesn't guarantee success,
but without it you stand no chance."*

*This is a practice story and illustrates the commitment dedication
and determination required for individuals to take their skills to
the next level.*

Bill Sharman is a name which has been forgotten in the parlance of today's NBA, however in the early years of professional basketball he was one of its brightest stars. A WW II Navy veteran, he graduated from the University of Southern California; where he was an All American basketball player and the first baseman on their 1948 National Championship baseball team.

He played from 1951-1961 with the Boston Celtics and teamed up with Bob Cousy forming, what remains one of the finest back court tandems in NBA history. He was a four time NBA Champ, an eight time NBA All Star and a four time member of the All NBA first team. He was named to the NBA's 25th and 50th Anniversary Teams and he was elected to the National Basketball Hall of Fame as a player in 1976 and as a coach in 2004. His number 21 was retired by the Boston Celtics and hangs from TD Garden in Boston as it hung in the old "Garden" before.

He also played five years in the minor league system of the Brooklyn Dodgers; playing outfield and third base in the Dodger system. He made it to the AAA St. Paul Saints where he hit .293 in two seasons.

The best foul shooter of his era and still among the best who have ever played the game, Sharman led the NBA in free throw percentage a record seven times including five in a row. His mark of 93.2% shooting in a single season he held for over two decades and he still holds the record for having made 56 consecutive free throws in playoff competition.

A ferocious competitor and a tenacious defender, it is how he got there that exhibits his commitment to hard work and desire to improve by going the extra mile.

His method was simple. At the end of every practice, when everyone else had left the gym, Bill Sharman's work was about to begin. He would go to the free throw line and he would not leave the gym until he sank 100 consecutive foul shots! That's right 100 consecutive foul shots. There were many a time when he would be at 93 or 96 and he would miss. And he always went back to 1!!!

Bill Sharman is still ranked 11th on the all-time list for free throw shooting percentage, and he has been among the all-time leaders longer than anyone in basketball history!

So think about what part of your game you want to improve? What part of your game do you want to be better at? Which part of your game do you want to be the best at? And then, like Bill Sharman, set your sites and DO NOT STOP until you have gone the extra mile....and beyond!

https://www.youtube.com/watch?v=b1SDWgF5Wnw

57. ALWAYS WORKING TO GET BETTER

STEVE CARLTON—TO TEACH THE WORLD
TO THROW A SLIDER.

This is a practice story to help players uncover their personal drive to improve.

On January 12, 1994, Steve Carlton was inducted into the Major League Baseball Hall of Fame in Cooperstown, NY. Despite not speaking to reporters for 20 years he received 436 of 455 votes (95.6%). At the time of his induction, only Ty Cobb, Hank Aaron, Johnny Bench and Tom Seaver had received a higher percentages of the vote totals and in 2016 he was still the 13th highest on that all-time list.

Carlton broke in as a 20 year old with the St. Louis Cardinals in 1965. The young southpaw showed a lot of promise featuring a fastball and curve in his repertoire. The ace of the Cardinals staff was the dominant Bob Gibson who threw a wicked slider and after watching Gibson dominate in 1968, the young "Lefty" decided to add the slider to his arsenal.

The testing ground was Japan where the 1968 National League Champion Cardinals traveled following the season. And the hitter was none other than Sadaharu Oh; Japans all-time home run leader, 868 of them in fact. Oh had taken Carlton deep and when he came around again, Carlton decided the time had come to unveil his new pitch. "I decided to try an intimidate him" he said. "So I threw it right at his ribs...and when he stepped back I knew I had him." Carlton struck out the Japanese star from that point on, Steve Carlton and his slider would become one. His long time catcher Tim McCarver said, "His slider broke so quick and so late that hitters thought it was a strike and it wasn't."

The rest, as the saying goes, is history. And what a history. Steve Carlton pitched 24 seasons compiling 329 career wins (11th all-time). He had six 20 win seasons, four times leading the National League in wins. Five times he led the league in strikeouts with a high of 310 in 1972. He was the first lefty to strike out 4000 batters and his 4,136 punch outs is fourth all-time. He five times led the league in innings pitched, three times in complete games and he once was the ERA champ. He was the first pitcher in history to garner four Cy Young Awards.

Perhaps his most remarkable feat was his 27-10 year in 1972. His 27 wins was accompanied by a league leading 1.97 ERA. This came on a team that was 59-97 and finished 37 ½ games out of first place. Carlton won an astounding 46% of the Phillies games; and when Cooperstown came a calling, Steve "Lefty" Carlton took his rightful place among the game's all-time greats.

And all because he wanted to get better, he wanted to improve, he wanted to take his game to the next level! In an interview with ESPN's Roy Firestone, Carlton was asked this question; "What do you think your purpose is on this earth?" Through a wry smile Carlton replied, "To teach the world how to throw a slider."

What part of your game can you improve? What can you add to your game that is not yet there? How much better do you want to get? What will you do to take your game to the next level? What about this game would you like to teach the world to do?

https://www.youtube.com/watch?v=R7xsdUOEnvg

http://hardballtalk.nbcsports.com/2012/03/02/video-of-the-day-steve-carlton-was-born-to-throw-a-slider/

58. MAKING AN ADJUSTMENT

SANDY KOUFAX

This is a practice story about taking instruction and applying adjustments. It is about keeping an open mind and actively listening to a coach or instructor who is "repeating" something a player has heard before. You never know when a player will have his personal epiphany.

It was June 24, 1955 in County Stadium, Milwaukee when a 19 year old Sandy Koufax made his major league debut with the Brooklyn Dodgers. The Braves were leading 7-1 in the fifth when manager Walter Alston decided it was time to have a look at this left-handed pitcher with so much promise. His debut turned out to be a microcosm of his entire career. The first batter he faced was Braves shortstop Johnny Logan who welcomed him to the big leagues with a single. Hall of Fame third baseman Eddie Matthews followed with a ground ball back to Koufax who committed an error on his throw to second. Hank Aaron then walked on four pitches to load the bases. Koufax then struck out Bobby Thompson on a 3-2 pitch and induced power hitting first baseman Joe Adcock to hitting a double play ground ball to short to end the inning leaving Koufax and the Dodgers unscathed. The following inning the Braves went 1, 2, 3 with a ground out, a pop to center and a strike out, dispensed in 13 pitches.

Signed as a 'Bonus Baby" major league rules prohibited the Dodgers from sending him to the minors for two years, and thus the young southpaw learned the game from the at the major league level, never spending a day in the minors. He threw only 100 innings those first two years.

His first six years he pitched in 174 games, starting 103 of them. His record was 36-40 and his ERA was 4.06. Despite showing remarkable promise, his untamed wildness appeared it would always remain so and the number of Sandy Koufax doubters was increasing.

It was on a bus ride in 1961 during spring training in Vero Beach, Florida that it all changed. Sharing the ride with Dodger backup catcher Norm Sherry, they talked of Sandy's enigmatic performance. Sherry said simply, "Sandy, you could solve your control problem if you'd just try to throw the ball easier…Just get it over the plate… You've still got enough swift on it to get the hitters out." This was a message Koufax had heard before but it never resonated more than on this day. "In the past I'd go out there and, every pitch I threw, I'd try to throw harder than the last one," Koufax said, "From then on I tried to throw strikes and make them hit the ball. The whole difference was control. Not just controlling the ball, but controlling myself, too."

The realization that being in control of himself was directly related to being in control of his pitches changed Sandy Koufax forever!

This was not the first time that Koufax had heard this however, it was at that particular moment, on that particular day that it hit home and he understood its meaning.

It was there that the transformation began and Sandy Koufax went from prospect to superstar. He ultimately would earn the nickname "The Left Hand of God" as he went on to become one of the most dominant pitchers in the entire history of the game.

From 1961 until his premature retirement following the 1966 season, Sandy Koufax went 119-47 for an astounding .717 winning percentage. He had the lowest ERA in the National League for five straight years, three of them leading the majors. Three times he won the pitching triple-crown, and three times he struck out 300+ batters in a season with a record 382 in 1965. He also became the first pitcher to hurl three and four no-hitters. He was elected into the Hall of Fame in 1972.

Pirates Hall of Fame outfielder Willie Stargell said that trying to hit Koufax was like eating soup with a fork!

Many baseball historians will argue that Sandy Koufax had five seasons of dominance that was unmatched in baseball history. And it all came about because he simply made an adjustment. Men many times you will hear coaches repeat things to you; do not let yourself tune them out! Sometimes it takes hearing or seeing something many times before you come to understand it and then implement it. Keep your minds open, listen, take in what you're hearing and don't be afraid to implement it. Don't be afraid to make that adjustment. Never a better time than today to make the adjustment and get better!

https://espn.go.com/sportscentury/features/00016063.html

https://www.youtube.com/watch?v=g7ELwiiQSTY

59. CONSISTENT WINNER, ALWAYS HUNTED

EDWIN MOSES— STRIVE FOR CONSISTENCY

This is a story to use when your team is enjoying a successful season. It is useful in helping them to maintain focus and understand that as a result of their success they have to prepare to receive the best that every opponent has to offer. They are playing with a target on their backs. This story can be a practice story or pregame before a dangerous opponent.

There is no athlete in the history of competition who has had more of a stranglehold on an athletic event than Edwin Moses. No one has ever performed with more consistency to win over and over again, event after event, year after year. He was 6'-2" and 170 lbs. and his event was the 400 meter hurdles.

A hurdler out of Morehouse College and a physics major, he became a world record holder in the 400 hurdles, using only 13 strides between each one. As a world record holder he lost to West Germany's Harald Schmid in August of 1977. Two weeks later he faced Schmid again and beat him by 15 meters, vaulting him into a streak that is unsurpassed in the history of sports and competition. It would be nine years, nine months and nine days before Edwin Moses would lose another race.

He went nearly a decade before losing to; 122 straight victories! There were no fall downs, no disqualifications, and no pulled muscles. Through cold days, wet days, hot days and dry days, Edwin Moses was there, competing and winning! Encapsulated within were two world records, three world cup titles, a world championship gold medal and two Olympic golds.

His streak came to an end in June of 1987 when he lost to fellow

American Danny Harris; following which he won another 10 more races in a row. When he was 33 years old he attempted to capture his third gold medal and although he ran his best time ever, it was only good enough for a bronze medal.

For a decade, Edwin Moses was at the peak of his sport and hunted by everyone. We have enjoyed a lot of success of late. We too are hunted, we will see everyone's best pitcher and we will get everybody's best effort. It is the price we pay for being a consistent winner. Savor your victories men for we, like Moses, have to stay focused, consistent and get the best of us to prevail. Pitch by pitch, every at bat and every ball that comes your way.

https://www.youtube.com/watch?v=WRErJHil7nQ

60. POTENTIAL...NEVER WON A THING!

IT TAKES SO MUCH MORE.

Potential- Adjective, having or showing the capacity to develop in the future. Noun, latent qualities or abilities that may be developed and lead to future success or usefulness. This is a story that can be used in a practice setting or streamlined for a pre-game story.

Potential: it is unexposed ability, reserved power, untapped strength, unused success, dormant gifts, hidden talents or latent power. It is the sum total of who you can be but have yet to reveal. It is who you may choose to be or not be. Potential is a blessing and potential is a curse.

The MLB draft began in 1965. Since that time 51 players were chosen the first overall pick. Many we have heard of and many are playing today: Bryce Harper and David Price are performing at exceptional levels in the big leagues. But how about Matt Bush, Brien Taylor or Steven Chilcott? All names lost to history who never played a big league game. In fact, in 2016 Ken Griffey Jr. became the first overall number one pick to be inducted into the Major League Baseball Hall of Fame in Cooperstown!

Football has their fair share of "Potentials" who vanished from the scene. The 1982 New England Patriots made DE Ken Sims out of Texas the overall number one pick. What followed for Sims was eight years of mediocrity garnering only 17 sacks in 74 NFL games. Known for showing little interest in practicing or learning to improve; Sims earned the nickname "Game Day," but not for reasons you'd imagine. He explained away his lack of interest in practice by saying "I'll be there on game day." A promise he rarely kept. In 1999, the Browns made Kentucky quarterback Tim Couch the coveted first pick. The result was a five year career in which he threw 64 touchdown passes and 67 interceptions. And in 2007, Oakland tapped LSU quarterback JaMarcus Russell at number one and following a number of less than mediocre seasons he was released. Russell attempted a 2013 comeback which fell short. He has been called by some pundits "the greatest bust in NFL history."

No tale tells the story of squandered potential more than basketball's Earl "The Goat" Manigault. 'Goat" was legendary on the asphalt courts of Harlem in the late 1950s and early 60's. Playing on the streets with NBA legends Connie Hawkins, Earl Monroe and Kareem Abdul Jabbar, "Goat" was as good as any of them and in some eyes, better! He never played beyond high school yet in 1995 Kareem was asked who was the best player he ever played with or against in all his basketball career and without hesitation the NBA great responded, "that's easy....Goat!"

Gentlemen, limitless potential is an ingredient to success but it is not a requirement! It has never had an at bat, nor played a down. It has never grabbed a rebound or led a fast break and it has never taken the field. If you do not put forth the effort, the commitment, the dedication to cultivate your potential, it will add up to lackluster performances, unreached goals and broken dreams. For it is potential PLUS effort PLUS commitment PLUS dedication that equals success.

Mallozzi, Vincent M. (September 1995). "King Of Kings". SLAM Magazine.

61. THE NATIONAL ANTHEM

WHY AND HOW

Believe it or not, there is a correct way to stand for the National Anthem. Teaching your players how to stand for the Anthem will be worth all the time, energy and effort involved.

There is something within us about going last or being last. How many times have you heard the expression, "save the best for last"? And that is why we have chosen this story to end this book. For in the end when we examine why we all coach it boils down to three basic facts. First- that we understand that athletic endeavors are the greatest metaphor for life and coaching young people gives the opportunity to teach a wide range of life lessons. Two- our passion and love for the games. And three- in the end, our objective is to play a part in the formation of good citizens as we hand off America to its next generation.

The tradition of the National Anthem being played at a sporting event began on September 5, 1918. America was embroiled in the "Great War" (WW I) and the Boston Red Sox were playing the Chicago Cubs in the first game of the World Series. The season had been shortened as Major League Baseball was "releasing" their players to either fight or work in an "essential" industry. It was the bottom of the seventh inning when a marching band in attendance spontaneously broke in to the Star Spangled Banner. Babe Ruth was on the mound and he stopped his warm up pitches and placed his cap over his heart. The other players followed suit as did many men in the stands, thus giving birth to an American tradition. This was 13 years before Herbert Hoover signed the bill into law which officially made the Star Spangled Banner our National Anthem.

Protocol calls for players and coaches to stand at attention, cap in their right hand over their heart and their left hand in a closed fist resting in the small of their back. It is a simple process which, in fact, is fun to practice and it will also serve as a sign of total preparation!

The benefits of this exercise are many and they are immeasurable. As you are practicing this, you can teach your players the history of the National Anthem outlined above. You can inform them of the fact that 1.3 million Americans have died fighting under that flag and another three million have shed their blood; and in the stands behind them may well be someone who has lost a grandparent, a parent, a spouse or a child in war and the flag may be a reminder to them. We honor the flag to honor them.

Your team will take pride in their presentation for the anthem and you will hear their comments throughout the year which will illustrate that fact!

The biblical adage from Matthew tells us that "the last shall be first." This little exercise marks our last story for you. However make no mistake, that the most important mission for us as coaches is to educate, guide and mentor those in our charge by building character and modeling the responsibility of good citizenship. Nothing we do is more important!

History of Anthem

https://www.youtube.com/watch?v=CnRQ8-MMX28

Francis Scott Key

https://www.youtube.com/watch?v=iiVryYnzmdl

Joe Komaroski (L) and Raymond Sinibaldi (R) have been a part of Coach Craig Faulkner's Venice High School baseball program for a collective three decades. Their energy has coalesced to bring together this collection of motivational stories that Coach Faulkner began gathering 33 years ago.

CPSIA information can be obtained
at www.ICGtesting.com
Printed in the USA
LVOW12s0849010416
481697LV00001B/1/P